Contents

Acknowledgements

The text of the poems is taken from the Penguin English Texts edition, edited by A. J. Smith.

Richard Gill would like to acknowledge the significant contribution many of his students have made to his learning and understanding of this rewarding body of work. In particular, he would like to single out Fiona Chamberlain, Margaret Finch and David Roe for their input. Special thanks are also due to Olivia Schelts, who helped him to think through this revised edition. Richard Gill would also like to thank Victor Lee, Jan Doorly and Jenny Roberts for their constructive criticism and advice.

Editors

Dr Victor Lee, the series editor, read English at University College, Cardiff. He was later awarded his doctorate at the University of Oxford. He has taught at secondary and tertiary level, working at the Open University for 27 years. Victor Lee's experience as an examiner is very wide. He has been, for example, a Chief Examiner in English A-Level for three different boards, stretching over a period of more than 30 years.

Richard Gill was Head of English at Wyggeston and Queen Elizabeth I College in Leicester and now teaches adults for the WEA (Workers' Educational Association) and Leicester University. He has published books on Jane Austen, Shakespeare, Tennyson and Yeats as well as a book on the study of English Literature.

Foreword

Oxford Student Texts are specifically aimed at presenting poetry and drama to an audience studying English literature at an advanced level. Each text is designed as an integrated whole consisting of four main parts. The first part sets the scene by discussing the context in which the work was written. The most important part of the book is the poetry or play itself, and it is suggested that the student reads this first without consulting the Notes or other secondary sources. To encourage students to follow this advice, the Notes are placed together after the text, not alongside it. Where help is needed, the Notes and Interpretations sections provide it.

The Notes perform two functions. First, they provide information and explain allusions. Second (this is where they differ from most texts at this level), they often raise questions of central concern to the interpretation of the poems or play being dealt with, particularly in the general note placed at the beginning of each set of notes.

The fourth part, the Interpretations section, deals with major issues of response to the particular selection of poetry or drama. One of the major aims of this part of the text is to emphasize that there is no one right answer to interpretation, but a series of approaches. Readers are given guidance as to what counts as evidence, but in the end left to make up their own minds as to which are the most suitable interpretations, or to add their own.

In these revised editions, the Interpretations section now addresses a wider range of issues. There is a more detailed treatment of context and critical history, for example. The section contains a number of activity-discussion sequences, although it must be stressed that these are optional. Significant issues about the poetry or play are raised, and readers are invited to tackle activities before proceeding to the discussion section, where possible responses to the questions raised are considered. Their main function is to engage readers actively in the ideas of the text.

At the end of each text there is also a list of Essay Questions. Whereas the activity-discussion sequences are aimed at increasing understanding of the literary work itself, these tasks are intended to help explore ideas about the poetry or play after the student has completed the reading of the work and the studying of the Notes and Interpretations. These tasks are particularly helpful for coursework projects or in preparing for an examination.

Victor Lee *Series Editor*

John Donne in Context

Thinking about the context of Donne's poetry cannot be a matter of looking at the poems in terms of the events of the poet's life because, in most cases, it is not known with any certainty when the poems were written. Most of Donne's poems cannot be *directly* connected to his life. Context, therefore, must mean the intellectual, religious, social and artistic aspects of the times in which he lived.

A new world

The Good Morrow is a characteristic Donne poem: it opens dramatically; there is the vigour and emotional colour of a living voice and a bracing inventiveness of idea and imagery. There is also, in its mood and subject matter, the sense that the poet is living in a new world. He wakes up to the wonder of a beloved he has glimpsed but never possessed, and beyond the intimacy of the *one little room* (11) in which they lie, there is, with the help of maps, *new worlds* (12) to explore. This poem might be said to be in the spirit of the Renaissance.

As with many of the words we use to indicate periods of culture, 'Renaissance' was only used after the age it designated was over. 'Renaissance' now means that period of artistic and intellectual activity which drew inspiration from Ancient Greek and Roman culture and which began in fourteenth-century Italy and was influential throughout Europe until the seventeenth century. This meaning dates from 1845. In other words, Donne could not have said: 'I am a Renaissance poet.' Yet he was undoubtedly a poet who displayed a restless, exploratory spirit, which delighted in testing out ideas and questioning many accepted views. He was born into a culture that was re-thinking painting, sculpture, architecture, law, politics, religion, literature, philosophy and science. That culture, at once both exciting and frightening, was Donne's context. There is a line from his poem *An Anatomy of the World* (not included in this selection), which is much quoted as summarizing the disturbance created by new thinking: *And new philosophy calls all in doubt* (205). *Philosophy* here means learning in both the sciences and the arts.

Discovery

The second stanza of *The Good Morrow* creates the image of *sea-discoverers* going to *new worlds*. It is as if the horizons of the known world are extended as we read the line. Voyages were a feature of Donne's world. Routes to the Americas and the East were being opened up. People wrote about sea discoveries: a representative figure was Richard Hakluyt, who published *Divers Voyages* in 1582 and *Voyages made into Florida* in 1587. Sea discoveries are central to Shakespeare's play *The Tempest* of 1611.

Sea journeys provide the occasion and the imagery for a number of Donne's poems. For example, '*Sweetest love*' and *A Hymn to Christ, at the Author's last going into Germany* arise from the poet going on a journey. Donne's imagery reflects three ways in which sea journeys were important in his time.

There is language concerned with gaining land and establishing colonies. In *Elegy 19* Donne puns (plays on words that have the same sounds but different meanings) on a newly discovered territory: *America, my new found land* (27).

Trade by sea and land gave many English people a taste for rare and precious things. Trade with the East is the subject of the line from *The Sun Rising*: *both th'Indias of spice and mine* (17). His beloved is even more precious than those much sought-after goods.

There was also the sheer sense of adventure and the desire to plot a course through strange regions. In *Hymn to God my God, in my Sickness* Donne says of his bed (his possible death-bed) that it is *my south-west discovery* (9). *Discovery* means a new route or sea passage to a desired destination. The lure of many kinds of adventures is felt throughout Donne's work.

Compasses and maps

Sea-discovery led to the invention and improvement of scientific instruments. Compasses (what we now call dividers) were needed to plot a sea course on a chart. Hence, it might be appropriate (though still arrestingly strange) that in his poem about restraining emotions upon parting, *A Valediction: forbidding Mourning*, Donne turns to compasses for an image of lovers divided though never separated. In his *Hymn to God my God, in my Sickness* the image of mapmaking fittingly leads to that of the sea journey. His *physicians* have become *cosmographers* and he, their patient, is *their map* (6–7), which shows his passage, his *south-west discovery* (9), to death.

Might the image of maps tell us something about Donne? Is it that he is a brave adventurer? There may also be the suggestion that his poetry is about self-discovery and that the image of maps is used to explore where and who he is.

An emblem from Henry Peacham's *Minerva Britanna*, showing compasses. Note also the stars and the dial, both of which can be used in plotting a journey

A portrait of John Donne as a young man. Perhaps he consciously poses as the amorous poet?

Medicine

Donne's poems are dramatically situated between extremes. There is an aspiration towards a perfect world as in the *dialogue of one* (74) between two souls in *The Ecstasy*. At the other extreme there are those poems in which the poet turns away in cynical disgust from a world that is frustratingly imperfect. *Love's Alchemy* is an example.

Health and sickness are two of Donne's extreme states. In *The Ecstasy* he dwells, as he does in several poems, on the *fast balm* (6) that, by holding the body together, prevents it from decaying. In *A Fever* he uses the idea that a feverish state is fuelled by *much corruption* (19). Illness is the result of an imbalance between the elements that constitute us. He closes *The Good Morrow* with the contemporary idea (also found in Shakespeare) that *What ever dies, was not mixed equally* (19), and then draws the conclusion that if the love he and his beloved shares is *one* (20), then *none can die* (21).

In Donne's time, exploratory thought was often conducted by means of parallels and correspondences. Features found in one area of study were expected to be present in another. Thus, as balm prevented human decay, so in nature as a whole it performed the same function. In that dark meditation upon death and negativity, *A Nocturnal upon S. Lucy's Day, being the shortest day*, the balm that keeps the natural world in being is being drunk by the ailing earth: *The general balm th' hydroptic earth hath drunk* (6). Negation dominates: his beloved is dead, *The world's whole sap is sunk* (5), and the poet feels that he is the *epitaph* (9) of this decay.

In Donne's day, scientific or technical language worked on a number of levels. This can be seen in Donne's use of the medical idea of dropsy, introduced into *A Nocturnal upon S. Lucy's Day, being the shortest day*. Dropsy or hydropsy was excessive thirst. In *Elegy 4* (6) the meaning is medical; in *Elegy 16* it is a metaphor for a longing for alcohol (42) and in *Holy Sonnet 17* it stands for the soul's unsatisfied desire for God (8). Perhaps that one word reveals a lot about Donne. He is a poet of insatiable desire.

Anatomy

The Damp opens with the poet imagining his own autopsy. In lines that depend upon monosyllabic bluntness and the chilly tone established by *curiosity*, he imagines the weird scene of his friends gathering to open up his body:

> **When I am dead, and doctors know not why,**
> **And my friends' curiosity**
> **Will have me cut up to survey each part**

This is decidedly Renaissance. Anatomy theatres were established throughout Europe (they can still be seen in Italy at Bologna and Padua), where students of anatomy could view, as in a playhouse, what lies hidden beneath the skin. For something as intimate and secretive as the inside of the body, anatomy was a very public practice. The probing of the anatomists – distinguishing muscles, cartilages, tendons – provided a language for analysis and examination. The word 'anatomy', meaning the dissection of the body, was first used in 1541 and by 1569 the word also meant analysis or detailed examination. Donne in this sense is an anatomical poet; he probes and analyses ideas and experiences. What, we may ask, is being analysed in *The Damp*? Is the subject of this curiously unemotional poem female or male power?

Because the practice of anatomy was new in the sixteenth century, it has a daring feel about it. The anatomist was like the sea-discoverer venturing into hitherto unvisited regions. But some of the ideas mentioned above about medicine were older. For instance, the idea of balm derives from the Swiss physician and chemist Paracelsus, (1493–1541), and when in *The Ecstasy* there is mention of souls containing a *Mixture of things* (34), Donne is using an idea that goes back to Aristotle (384–322 BC).

Astronomy

We misunderstand what we have come to call the Renaissance if we think that all its ideas were new. This is particularly evident in the case of Astronomy, the science that dominated the sixteenth century. Astronomy was a clear case of the new philosophy calling all in doubt. From the advantage of our knowledge, the issues seem easy, but to understand the excitement and anxiety of Donne's time we have to remember that nobody had certain knowledge. The debates about the stars in Christopher Marlowe's *Doctor Faustus* are, to us, a puzzling mish-mash of false ideas, but to Marlowe's (and Donne's) audiences they were thoughts about vexingly puzzling matters.

The received view of the universe was geocentric – the Earth was at the centre of things, and all the other heavenly bodies – sun, moon, stars and planets – revolved around it. This view of the universe as an enclosed system derived from Ptolemy (100–c.178), a Greek astronomer, whose *Almagest* was closely studied in the fourteenth and fifteenth centuries. Chaucer's clever student, Nicholas in *The Miller's Tale*, has an *Almagest*.

Ptolemy's picture of the universe (or extended and elaborated versions of it) was of a series of spheres or concentric globes, in which the planets and stars were located. Donne uses this idea in *Love's Growth*, where concentric spheres become an image of new loves added to what already exists:

> Those like so many spheres, but one heaven make,
> For, they are all concentric unto thee
>
> (23–4)

The common Christian belief in Donne's time was that the Earth, and all below the moon, had been damaged by the Fall (the disobedience of Adam and Eve) so was a place of corruption and decay, hence the *Dull sublunary lovers* (13) of *A Valedicion: forbidding Mourning*. But beyond the moon all was perfect, and as the spheres moved within each other a most miraculous music – the music of the spheres – was made. This was inaudible to human ears, so Donne is mocking, when in *Love's Alchemy* he sneers at the lover's claim that it is only the mind that marries. This, he says, is as absurd as claiming to hear in the rough music of a wedding feast *the spheres* (22).

The traditional view, going back to Aristotle, was that the stars and planets (they were not sharply distinguished until Galileo studied them) were moved from within by a force or intelligence, which was something like an angel. This proved to be a rich image for Donne. When in *The Ecstasy* he tries to find a role for the body, he uses the image of the soul as the intelligence that moves its sphere: *we are/The intelligences, they the sphere* (51–2).

A star could be deflected, but beyond the spheres lay what was secure from change or wavering – the *primum mobile*, the first mover and cause of all the movement within the universe. The *primum mobile*, first imagined by Aristotle, came to be associated (though not actually identified) with God. *Good Friday, 1613. Riding Westward* opens with a complex passage in which erring souls are compared to a deflected star, which is *Subject to foreign motions* (4). Nevertheless, souls still reach after *their first mover* (8).

New learning, old learning and poetry

References to Astronomy in Donne's poetry show that he was at home with the 'old' view of the world. But scientific understanding was changing. The geocentric (earth-centred) view gave way to a heliocentric (sun-centred) picture. In 1543 Copernicus argued that the Earth and planets revolved round the sun. His views were not immediately adopted, partly because in those days they were extremely difficult to prove. A number of serious mathematicians still held to the geocentric view. It took over sixty years for the heliocentric view to prevail, and by then it had been modified.

Copernicus argued that the planets revolved round the sun in perfect circles; Kepler, whose work Donne probably knew, argued in 1609 that planetary paths were elliptical. Galileo used his telescope or, as he would have called it, his glass. His published work of 1610, *Sidereus Nuncius*, distinguished between planets and stars.

There was much critical debate in the twentieth century about where Donne stood with regard to the new knowledge. Those who saw him as an intellectual and personal adventurer argued that he was as comfortable in the 'new world' as he was in the beds of his many lovers. Others pointed out his consistent appeal to a pre-Copernican view of the Earth. (There is a discussion of the debate in Frank Kermode's essay on William Empson, a strong advocate of the adventurer view of Donne, in the book *An Appetite for Poetry*, 1989.)

In the light of this brief discussion of old and new learning, what is to be made of Donne's poetry?

- Perhaps the first thing that should be said is that Donne might be seen as an adventurous man of a new age, not because he supported scientific views that have become established (he did not) but because he introduced scientific, technical and scholarly debate into his verse. To put it simply: it is not what he says that makes him a man of his time but the fact that he says it at all. What feels new, sometimes breath-takingly so, is the way he seizes ideas and makes them the material of his poetry.

- Second, there *is* a feel of the new in some of his remarks. He can, for instance, be dismissive of Alchemy. Compared to the reality of a mutually shared love, he says that *all wealth* is *alchemy* (*The Sun Rising*, 24). Alchemy was a sort of chemistry that, among its many aims, hoped to turn ordinary metals into gold. Love, by contrast, is real wealth.

- Third, it should be said that when nobody knew the answers, writing tended to mix what we now see as the old and new views. Likewise Donne, when he chooses, can both dismiss Alchemy and write of intelligences directing the planets. He is not alone in such mixing. Kepler's *Harmonices Mundi* of 1619 contains very important mathematics about the revolution of the planets and a refined version of the music of the spheres.

- Fourth, Donne uses knowledge by turning it into figures of speech about thoughts and experiences. In Donne scientific language is used comparatively. When at the close of *The Sun Rising* he advances stupendous claims for the nature of the love he and his beloved share he uses astronomical language:

> Shine here to us, and thou art everywhere;
> This bed thy centre is, these walls, thy sphere.
> (29–30)

This is akin to the old language of spheres centred on the Earth, but with sprightly impudence Donne makes their bed the centre of all things. He is not referring to scientific beliefs. Rather, he is using them figuratively to think through his experiences.

- Fifth, there are aspects of the new learning that are not prominent in Donne. He is, for instance, sparing in his classical references. Unlike, say, Christopher Marlowe, Donne does not frequently refer to the myths of Greece and Rome. Unlike many of his contemporaries, he was not strongly influenced by the Roman poet, Ovid, whose *Metamorphoses* is concerned with myths of physical transformation. By contrast, the Bible is an important source of ideas and images for Donne.

Changes in religion

The religion of Western Europe in the sixteenth and seventeenth centuries was a matter of daily conduct and fierce dispute. Virtually everybody engaged in public worship, and religious allegiance shaped moral, social and political behaviour. If some twenty-first century readers have a problem with this aspect of Donne's context, it is because in most contemporary western society religion is rarely regarded as a matter of supreme importance. Although there are, of course, exceptions.

Throughout Donne's life, England was coming to terms with the consequences of the Reformation. Unlike the word 'Renaissance', 'Reformation' was a contemporary term, its first recorded usage being 1563. The word 'Reformation' denotes a long and complex history of religious conflict that led to the establishment of the Church of England and, in mainland Europe, the Protestant churches that followed Martin Luther and John Calvin. Rome also changed. The Council of Trent (1545–63) revised practices and doctrines, a process called the Counter-Reformation.

The causes of the English Reformation are still debated. Scholars try to balance the relative importance of politics (Henry VIII wanted a divorce), the desire for reform (the Lollards, an influential fringe group, were discontented with the Church) and the evident devotion of the people to their Church (the intense devotion of churchgoers is called 'lay piety'). In England the impetus of the Reformation certainly had a political dimension. Henry VIII, a Renaissance monarch, wanted a divorce, and as the Pope would not grant him one, he established the Church of England as a separate body with the monarch as its head or, to use a slightly later term, 'supreme governor'. This was consistent with his desire to extend monarchical rule.

Although Henry was fiercely orthodox, he was unable to control the extent of the change, so the Mass was translated from Latin into English and the monasteries were dissolved between 1536 and 1539. Later, statues of the saints were destroyed, wall paintings in church were whitewashed and the conduct of services became plainer with the priest wearing solemn black rather than coloured vestments. The emphasis moved to preaching and away from the sacrifice of the Mass. English religion became more earnest (the very devout were often called 'the godly'), and, in terms of its liturgy, less dramatic.

Henry VIII was staunchly Catholic to the last. There are stories that on his death-bed he prayed to Our Lady of Walsingham (Walsingham being the Norfolk town, where Mary, the Mother of God, was venerated). He must have been typical of many who, in their hearts, could not let the 'old religion', as it came to be called, go. Many remained obedient to the Church of Rome. One such was Donne's mother, born Elizabeth Heywood. The Heywoods were related by marriage to Sir Thomas More, who had died for his faith, and two of Donne's uncles, Ellis and Jasper, became Jesuit priests. (The Jesuits were an order of priests, founded in 1534, dedicated to defending the Roman Church and converting the heathen.) Donne received a Catholic education, so, when in 1607 he was invited to enter into religious controversy on behalf of the Church of England against the Church of Rome, he knew from the inside what it was he was criticizing. In 1615 he was ordained a priest in the Church of England, and in 1621 was made Dean of St. Paul's Cathedral, London, a post he held to his death. He was one of the most admired preachers of his age.

Religious controversy may lead us to forget the significant things that the Roman Catholic Church and the Church of

England had in common. Perhaps the most significant for a poet was that both were increasingly concerned to nurture the 'inner life'. Spiritual reading was important to both churches as a way of nourishing the soul, so that believers could develop appropriate attitudes to the worship of God and the daily practice of religion. Thus, in both churches an awareness of how God's Spirit works in the heart and mind became a central concern. Donne's *Holy Sonnets* can be read as explorations of what it feels like to be a believer. Louis Martz's study *The Poetry of Meditation* plots the influence this movement in spiritual reading had on seventeenth-century literature.

Neo-Platonism

The influence of Neo-Platonism can be felt in sixteenth and seventeenth-century literature, because Plato's thinking about knowledge and the nature of the soul permeated the assumptions of the age.

Plato was a Greek philosopher (427–347 BC), whose various works have his teacher, Socrates, as the central character. Through dialogue, stories and elusively poetic passages of speculation, Plato attempted to persuade people to reflect on the nature of their experience and through this to come to an understanding of how we know what we know. Neo-Platonism is a convenient term for denoting thought in the Platonic tradition. The word is often associated with the speculative element in Platonic thinking.

Fundamental to Plato and Neo-Platonism is that things are not as they seem. Reality, in other words, is not to be confused with appearance. An elephant seen at 300 metres will look small, but small it is not. Knowledge, for Plato, was always a struggle to pass beyond the confusions of appearance and see things for what they actually were.

The search for the real turned on the nature of the soul. Plato proposed that appearances constitute an unreal world, like shadows cast on the sides of a cave. The one who wishes to know must, so to speak, turn away from shadows and gaze on the sun itself. In trying to see things for what they are, we realize that things form classes or categories. Greyhounds are very different from poodles, but we see both of them are dogs. How can we understand why we know this? Perhaps, speculated Plato, the soul, before it was born into this world, saw the real (or Ideal) Forms of every object, so our knowing is a kind of remembering of what the soul once saw. As in the case of trying to see the sun, the soul must make an intellectual search for the Ideal Forms.

Plato influenced ideas about love. To love the soul rather than the body is called platonic love. *The Undertaking*, the theme of which is loving *loveliness within* (13), is sometimes titled *Platonic Love*. In the light of this thought, kissing could be seen as a spiritual activity, as in *The Relic* (27–8). In a kiss, the soul comes to the lips in order to leave the body, so a kiss unites souls. The Renaissance scholar Baldesar Castiglione (1478–1529) wrote in his highly influential work on the manners and culture of court life, *The Courtier* (1528), that 'all chaste lovers desire a kiss as a union of souls'. (Translated by George Bull, Penguin, 1967.)

As with Astronomy, these ideas were poetically useful to Donne. In *Air and Angels* he understands the glimpses he has had of his beloved in other women in terms of the Platonic distinction between appearance and reality.

Platonism has links with religion in that it believes in a world beyond that detected by the senses. It also has links with science and learning, because Plato believed that the world, or reality, was rational and orderly and that therefore mathematics (increasingly important in Astronomy) was a guide to how things are.

London and city life

Donne was born and died in London. He is not a poet of nature; many readers have commented that the beauties of the natural world rarely delight him. His is a social world, a world, as he says in *The Canonization*, of *towns, courts* (44).

Many of the poems are set indoors. *Elegy 4* is about maintaining private space; it revels in the pleasures of lovers' meetings, presumably in her chamber, and the (almost equal?) pleasure of keeping those meetings secret. Bedrooms are the settings of *The Dream*, *The Good Morrow* and *The Sun Rising*. *The Apparition* is a dramatic and comic imagining of the ghost of the rejected lover coming to the bed, which he never reached in life, and finding, in the flickering glare of a guttering candle, a girl sweating with fear and a lover sound asleep.

Occasionally, there are glimpses of the affluent world of the London professional classes. *Elegy 19* is very detailed on the inviting layers of a rich woman's clothes. There are curtains round the bed in *The Sun Rising*, thumb rings exchanged by lovers appear in *A Jet Ring Sent*, and in *Hymn to God my God, in my Sickness* musicians, no doubt nervously, tune their instruments before entering a room to play. Musical performance, another feature of the wealthy classes, is the subject of *The Triple Fool*, a poem in which the poet has to re-live the passions he put into one of his poems, when he hears it sung, in all probability to the accompaniment of a lute.

This is the world of successful people, the people for whom Donne may have consciously written. Yet he is distant from one particular world – the Court of the Monarch. Ambitious young men sought to establish themselves in the Court, and, by tradition, many of them wrote poetry. In the early sixteenth century two poets – Henry Howard, Earl of Surrey (1517–47) and Sir Thomas Wyatt (1503–42) – were both courtiers. But Donne sometimes adopts the stance of the outsider, perhaps the man of disappointed ambition or the critic of excess. Is there, for instance, an impatience with courtly frivolity in *Go tell court-huntsmen, that the King will ride* (*The Sun Rising*, 7)? Perhaps there is a biographical element; Donne never achieved a place in the Court.

Poetry

One of the most important contexts is that of poetry itself. Donne lived in a culture that observed the elaborate conventions of a love poetry that derived from the Italian poet Petrarch (1304–74) and his followers. A literary convention is a kind of agreement between writer and reader as to how to understand what is happening in literature. Thus, in the Petrarchan tradition a beautiful woman was, by convention, blonde with dazzling eyes, sweet breath, a soft voice and smooth gliding movements. When these details appear in literature, they should be read not so much as a description of an actual woman but as an indication that she is devastatingly beautiful.

Many of Donne's love poems open with a reference to a Petrarchan convention. Sometimes the setting is pastoral; that is to say, the lovers are placed in a country setting, as in *The Ecstasy*. By convention, pastoral settings suggest an ideal world, where, in beautiful surroundings, lovers live care-free lives. Lovers also perform outlandish acts of daring to please a beloved, as in the opening of *Song: Go, and catch a falling star*. To part from a beloved is like death (*The Expiration*). A beloved so controls a lover's feelings that her picture is found in his heart (*The Damp*, 4). The death of a beloved takes away the soul of the world (*A Fever*, 8). Excessive sighs and tears are characteristically Petrarchan. There are *sweet salt tears* in *The Anniversary* (16), *unkindly kind* weeping in *Song: Sweetest love* (27) and *tear-floods* and *sigh-tempests* in *A Valediction: forbidding Mourning* (6). The Petrarchan lover is often melancholic (see illustration on p. 17).

Petrarchan conventions extend to the difficulties of love. An unresponsive woman is often called cruel. In *The Apparition*, the lover has been killed by a woman's scorn. The difficulties of love lend particular force to the word 'mistress'. In addressing beloveds as mistresses, poets were working with a medieval tradition in which lovers regarded the one they loved as exercising power over them and whom, therefore, they had to serve.

It is not always easy to judge what Donne's attitude to Petrarchan conventions was. He appears to accept them in *The Expiration* and *Song: Sweetest love*, yet in others he is clearly mocking. In *The Canonization*, for instance, he appears to enjoy the absurd idea that excessive sighing can influence the weather: *What merchant's ships have my sighs drowned?* (11). Perhaps the test is whether he sounds Petrarchan. And if he does not, is this to do with features that characterize Donne's poetry? Many poems written under the influence of Petrarch are smooth and mellifluous, whereas Donne's tone is conversational and his rhythms are irregular. This is an issue discussed in detail in the Interpretations section.

An unknown youth by Nicholas Hilliard. The youthful love-sick man is reminiscent of a Petrarchan lover

Songs and Sonnets

Air and Angels

Twice or thrice had I loved thee,
Before I knew thy face or name;
So in a voice, so in a shapeless flame,
Angels affect us oft, and worshipped be;
5   Still when, to where thou wert, I came,
Some lovely glorious nothing I did see,
    But since my soul, whose child love is,
Takes limbs of flesh, and else could nothing do,
    More subtle than the parent is
10   Love must not be, but take a body too,
    And therefore what thou wert, and who
       I bid love ask, and now
That it assume thy body, I allow,
And fix itself in thy lip, eye, and brow.

15   Whilst thus to ballast love, I thought,
And so more steadily to have gone,
With wares which would sink admiration,
I saw, I had love's pinnace overfraught,
    Every thy hair for love to work upon
20   Is much too much, some fitter must be sought;
    For, nor in nothing, nor in things
Extreme, and scatt'ring bright, can love inhere;
    Then as an angel, face and wings
Of air, not pure as it, yet pure doth wear,
25   So thy love may be my love's sphere;
      Just such disparity
As is 'twixt air and angels' purity,
'Twixt women's love, and men's will ever be.

The Anniversary

All kings, and all their favourites,
All glory of honours, beauties, wits,
The sun itself, which makes times, as they pass,
Is elder by a year, now, than it was
5   When thou and I first one another saw:
All other things, to their destruction draw,
    Only our love hath no decay;
This, no tomorrow hath, nor yesterday,
Running it never runs from us away,
10   But truly keeps his first, last, everlasting day.

Two graves must hide thine and my corse,
    If one might, death were no divorce,
Alas, as well as other princes, we,
(Who prince enough in one another be,)
15   Must leave at last in death, these eyes, and ears,
Oft fed with true oaths, and with sweet salt tears;
But souls where nothing dwells but love
(All other thoughts being inmates) then shall prove
This, or a love increased there above,
20   When bodies to their graves, souls from their graves
        remove.

And then we shall be throughly blessed,
    But we no more, than all the rest.
Here upon earth, we are kings, and none but we
Can be such kings, nor of such subjects be;
25   Who is so safe as we? where none can do
Treason to us, except one of us two.
    True and false fears let us refrain,
Let us love nobly, and live, and add again
Years and years unto years, till we attain
30   To write threescore, this is the second of our reign.

The Apparition

When by thy scorn, O murderess, I am dead,
And that thou think'st thee free
From all solicitation from me,
Then shall my ghost come to thy bed,
5   And thee, feigned vestal, in worse arms shall see;
Then thy sick taper will begin to wink,
And he, whose thou art then, being tired before,
Will, if thou stir, or pinch to wake him, think
     Thou call'st for more,
10   And in false sleep will from thee shrink,
And then poor aspen wretch, neglected thou
Bathed in a cold quicksilver sweat wilt lie
     A verier ghost than I;
What I will say, I will not tell thee now,
15   Lest that preserve thee; and since my love is spent,
I had rather thou shouldst painfully repent,
Than by my threatenings rest still innocent.

Break of Day

'Tis true, 'tis day, what though it be?
O wilt thou therefore rise from me?
Why should we rise, because 'tis light?
Did we lie down, because 'twas night?
5   Love which in spite of darkness brought us hither,
Should in despite of light keep us together.

Light hath no tongue, but is all eye;
If it could speak as well as spy,
This were the worst, that it could say,
10   That being well, I fain would stay,
And that I loved my heart and honour so,
That I would not from him, that had them, go.

Must business thee from hence remove?
Oh, that's the worst disease of love,
15   The poor, the foul, the false, love can
Admit but not the busied man.
He which hath business, and makes love, doth do
Such wrong, as when a married man doth woo.

The Canonization

For God's sake hold your tongue, and let me love,
    Or chide my palsy, or my gout,
My five grey hairs, or ruined fortune flout,
      With wealth your state, your mind with arts
        improve,
5   Take you a course, get you a place,
        Observe his Honour, or his Grace,
Or the King's real, or his stamped face
    Contemplate; what you will, approve,
    So you will let me love.

10 Alas, alas, who's injured by my love?
      What merchant's ships have my sighs drowned?
Who says my tears have overflowed his ground?
    When did my colds a forward spring remove?
      When did the heats which my veins fill
15   Add one more to the plaguy bill?
Soldiers find wars, and lawyers find out still
    Litigious men, which quarrels move,
    Though she and I do love.

Call us what you will, we are made such by love;
20   Call her one, me another fly,
We are tapers too, and at our own cost die,
    And we in us find the eagle and the dove,
      The phoenix riddle hath more wit
      By us; we two being one, are it.
25 So to one neutral thing both sexes fit
    We die and rise the same, and prove
    Mysterious by this love.

We can die by it, if not live by love,
    And if unfit for tombs and hearse
30   Our legend be, it will be fit for verse;
And if no piece of chronicle we prove,
        We'll build in sonnets pretty rooms;
        As well a well wrought urn becomes
The greatest ashes, as half-acre tombs,
35   And by these hymns, all shall approve
      Us canonized for love:

And thus invoke us; 'You whom reverend love
      Made one another's hermitage;
You, to whom love was peace, that now is rage;
40   Who did the whole world's soul contract, and
        drove
      Into the glasses of your eyes
      (So made such mirrors, and such spies,
That they did all to you epitomize,)
      Countries, towns, courts: beg from above
45   A pattern of your love!'

The Damp

When I am dead, and doctors know not why,
     And my friends' curiosity
Will have me cut up to survey each part,
When they shall find your picture in my heart,
5   You think a sudden damp of love
       Will through all their senses move,
And work on them as me, and so prefer
Your murder, to the name of massacre.

Poor victories; but if you dare be brave,
10   And pleasure in your conquest have,
First kill th' enormous giant, your Disdain,
And let th' enchantress Honour, next be slain,
       And like a Goth and Vandal rise,
       Deface records, and histories
15   Of your own arts and triumphs over men,
And without such advantage kill me then.

For I could muster up as well as you
       My giants, and my witches too,
Which are vast Constancy, and Secretness,
20   But these I neither look for, nor profess;
       Kill me as woman, let me die
       As a mere man; do you but try
Your passive valour, and you shall find then,
Naked you have odds enough of any man.

The Dream

Dear love, for nothing less than thee
Would I have broke this happy dream,
    It was a theme
For reason, much too strong for phantasy,
5   Therefore thou waked'st me wisely; yet
My dream thou brok'st not, but continued'st it:
Thou art so true, that thoughts of thee suffice,
To make dreams truths, and fables histories;
Enter these arms, for since thou thought'st it best,
10   Not to dream all my dream, let's act the rest.

As lightning, or a taper's light,
Thine eyes, and not thy noise waked me;
    Yet I thought thee
(For thou lov'st truth) an angel, at first sight,
15   But when I saw thou saw'st my heart,
And knew'st my thoughts, beyond an angel's art,
When thou knew'st what I dreamed, when thou
    knew'st when
Excess of joy would wake me, and cam'st then,
I must confess, it could not choose but be
20   Profane, to think thee anything but thee.

Coming and staying showed thee, thee,
But rising makes me doubt, that now,
    Thou art not thou.
That love is weak, where fear's as strong as he;
25   'Tis not all spirit, pure, and brave,
If mixture it of fear, shame, honour, have.
Perchance as torches which must ready be,
Men light and put out, so thou deal'st with me,
Thou cam'st to kindle, goest to come; then I
30   Will dream that hope again, but else would die.

The Ecstasy

Where, like a pillow on a bed,
    A pregnant bank swelled up, to rest
The violet's reclining head,
    Sat we two, one another's best;

5   Our hands were firmly cemented
        With a fast balm, which thence did spring,
Our eye-beams twisted, and did thread
        Our eyes, upon one double string;

So to' intergraft our hands, as yet
10   Was all our means to make us one,
And pictures in our eyes to get
        Was all our propagation.

As 'twixt two equal armies, Fate
        Suspends uncertain victory,
15   Our souls, (which to advance their state,
        Were gone out), hung 'twixt her, and me.

And whilst our souls negotiate there,
        We like sepulchral statues lay;
All day, the same our postures were,
20   And we said nothing, all the day.

If any, so by love refined,
        That he soul's language understood,
And by good love were grown all mind,
        Within convenient distance stood,

25   He (though he knew not which soul spake
        Because both meant, both spake the same)
    Might thence a new concoction take,
        And part far purer than he came.

    This ecstasy doth unperplex
30   (We said) and tell us what we love,
    We see by this, it was not sex,
        We see, we saw not what did move:

    But as all several souls contain
        Mixture of things, they know not what,
35   Love, these mixed souls doth mix again,
        And makes both one, each this and that.

    A single violet transplant,
        The strength, the colour, and the size,
    (All which before was poor, and scant,)
40   Redoubles still, and multiplies.

    When love, with one another so
        Interinanimates two souls,
    That abler soul, which thence doth flow,
        Defects of loneliness controls.

45   We then, who are this new soul, know,
        Of what we are composed, and made,
    For, th' atomies of which we grow,
        Are souls, whom no change can invade.

    But O alas, so long, so far
50   Our bodies why do we forbear?
    They are ours, though they are not we, we are
        The intelligences, they the sphere.

We owe them thanks, because they thus,
    Did us, to us, at first convey,
55 Yielded their forces, sense, to us,
    Nor are dross to us, but allay.

On man heaven's influence works not so,
    But that it first imprints the air,
So soul into the soul may flow,
60   Though it to body first repair.

As our blood labours to beget
    Spirits, as like souls as it can,
Because such fingers need to knit
    That subtle knot, which makes us man:

65 So must pure lovers' souls descend
    T' affections, and to faculties,
Which sense may reach and apprehend,
    Else a great prince in prison lies.

To our bodies turn we then, that so
70   Weak men on love revealed may look;
Love's mysteries in souls do grow,
    But yet the body is his book.

And if some lover, such as we,
    Have heard this dialogue of one,
75 Let him still mark us, he shall see
    Small change, when we'are to bodies gone.

The Expiration

So, so, break off this last lamenting kiss,
    Which sucks two souls, and vapours both away,
Turn thou ghost that way, and let me turn this,
    And let ourselves benight our happiest day,
5   We asked none leave to love; nor will we owe
        Any, so cheap a death, as saying, Go;

Go; and if that word have not quite killed thee,
    Ease me with death, by bidding me go too.
Oh, if it have, let my word work on me,
10   And a just office on a murderer do.
Except it be too late, to kill me so,
    Being double dead, going, and bidding, go.

A Fever

Oh do not die, for I shall hate
    All women so, when thou art gone,
That thee I shall not celebrate,
    When I remember, thou wast one.

5   But yet thou canst not die, I know,
    To leave this world behind, is death,
But when thou from this world wilt go,
    The whole world vapours with thy breath.

Or if, when thou, the world's soul, go'st,
10   It stay, 'tis but thy carcase then,
The fairest woman, but thy ghost,
        But corrupt worms, the worthiest men.

Oh wrangling schools, that search what fire
        Shall burn this world, had none the wit
15 Unto this knowledge to aspire,
        That this her fever might be it?

And yet she cannot waste by this,
        Nor long bear this torturing wrong,
For much corruption needful is
20   To fuel such a fever long.

These burning fits but meteors be,
        Whose matter in thee is soon spent.
Thy beauty, and all parts, which are thee,
        Are unchangeable firmament.

25 Yet 'twas of my mind, seizing thee,
        Though it in thee cannot perséver.
For I had rather owner be
        Of thee one hour, than all else ever.

The Flea

Mark but this flea, and mark in this,
How little that which thou deny'st me is;
Me it sucked first, and now sucks thee,
And in this flea, our two bloods mingled be;
5   Confess it, this cannot be said
A sin, or shame, or loss of maidenhead,
    Yet this enjoys before it woo,
        And pampered swells with one blood made of two,
And this, alas, is more than we would do.

10   Oh stay, three lives in one flea spare,
Where we almost, nay more than married are.
This flea is you and I, and this
Our marriage bed, and marriage temple is;
Though parents grudge, and you, we'are met,
15   And cloistered in these living walls of jet.
    Though use make you apt to kill me,
    Let not to this, self murder added be,
        And sacrilege, three sins in killing three.

Cruel and sudden, has thou since
20   Purpled thy nail, in blood of innocence?
In what could this flea guilty be,
Except in that drop which it sucked from thee?
Yet thou triumph'st, and say'st that thou
Find'st not thyself, nor me the weaker now;
25   'Tis true, then learn how false, fears be;
    Just so much honour, when thou yield'st to me,
        Will waste, as this flea's death took life from thee.

The Funeral

Whoever comes to shroud me, do not harm
      Nor question much
That subtle wreath of hair, which crowns my arm;
The mystery, the sign you must not touch,
5   For 'tis my outward soul,
Viceroy to that, which then to heaven being gone,
      Will leave this to control,
And keep these limbs, her provinces, from dissolution.

For if the sinewy thread my brain lets fall
10   Through every part,
Can tie those parts, and make me one of all;
These hairs which upward grew, and strength and art
      Have from a better brain,
Can better do it; except she meant that I
15   By this should know my pain,
As prisoners then are manacled, when they are
      condemned to die.

Whate'er she meant by it, bury it with me,
      For since I am
Love's martyr, it might breed idolatry,
20   If into others' hands these relics came;
      As 'twas humility
To afford to it all that a soul can do,
      So, 'tis some bravery,
That since you would save none of me, I bury some
      of you.

The Good Morrow

I wonder by my troth, what thou, and I
  Did, till we loved? were we not weaned till then,
But sucked on country pleasures, childishly?
  Or snorted we in the seven sleepers' den?
5   'Twas so; but this, all pleasures fancies be.
If ever any beauty I did see,
Which I desired, and got, 'twas but a dream of thee.

And now good morrow to our waking souls,
  Which watch not one another out of fear;
10 For love, all love of other sights controls,
  And makes one little room, an every where.
Let sea-discoverers to new worlds have gone,
Let maps to others, worlds on worlds have shown,
Let us possess one world, each hath one, and is one.

15 My face in thine eye, thine in mine appears,
  And true plain hearts do in the faces rest,
Where can we find two better hemispheres
  Without sharp north, without declining west?
What ever dies, was not mixed equally;
20 If our two loves be one, or, thou and I
Love so alike, that none do slacken, none can die.

A Jet Ring Sent

Thou art not so black, as my heart,
  Nor half so brittle, as her heart, thou art;
What wouldst thou say? Shall both our properties by
    thee be spoke,
  Nothing more endless, nothing sooner broke?

5   Marriage rings are not of this stuff;
  Oh, why should aught less precious, or less tough
Figure our loves? Except in thy name thou have bid it say,
  I am cheap, and naught but fashion, fling me away.

    Yet stay with me since thou art come,
10 Circle this finger's top, which didst her thumb.
Be justly proud, and gladly safe, that thou dost dwell
    with me,
  She that, oh, broke her faith, would soon break thee.

Lovers' Infiniteness

If yet I have not all thy love,
Dear, I shall never have it all,
I cannot breathe one other sigh, to move,
Nor can entreat one other tear to fall.
5 All my treasure, which should purchase thee,
Sighs, tears, and oaths, and letters I have spent,
Yet no more can be due to me,
Than at the bargain made was meant.
If then thy gift of love were partial,
10 That some to me, some should to others fall,
    Dear, I shall never have thee all.

35

Or if then thou gavest me all,
All was but all, which thou hadst then;
But if in thy heart, since, there be or shall
15   New love created be, by other men,
Which have their stocks entire, and can in tears,
In sighs, in oaths, and letters outbid me,
This new love may beget new fears,
For, this love was not vowed by thee.
20   And yet it was, thy gift being general,
The ground, thy heart is mine; whatever shall
     Grow there, dear, I should have it all.

Yet I would not have all yet,
He that hath all can have no more,
25   And since my love doth every day admit
New growth, thou shouldst have new rewards in
     store;
Thou canst not every day give me thy heart,
If thou canst give it, then thou never gav'st it:
Love's riddles are, that though thy heart depart,
30   It stays at home, and thou with losing sav'st it:
But we will have a way more liberal,
Than changing hearts, to join them, so we shall
     Be one, and one another's all.

Love's Alchemy

Some that have deeper digged love's mine than I,
Say, where his centric happiness doth lie:
   I have loved, and got, and told,
But should I love, get, tell, till I were old,
5 I should not find that hidden mystery;
    Oh, 'tis imposture all:
And as no chemic yet the elixir got,
   But glorifies his pregnant pot,
   If by the way to him befall
10 Some odoriferous thing, or medicinal,
    So, lovers dream a rich and long delight,
    But get a winter-seeming summer's night.

Our ease, our thrift, our honour, and our day,
Shall we, for this vain bubble's shadow pay?
15   Ends love in this, that my man,
Can be as happy as I can; if he can
Endure the short scorn of a bridegroom's play?
    That loving wretch that swears,
'Tis not the bodies marry, but the minds,
20 Which he in her angelic finds,
Would swear as justly, that he hears,
In that day's rude hoarse minstrelsy, the spheres.
Hope not for mind in women; at their best
   Sweetness and wit, they are but mummy, possessed.

Love's Growth

I scarce believe my love to be so pure
    As I had thought it was,
    Because it doth endure
Vicissitude, and season, as the grass;
5   Methinks I lied all winter, when I swore,
My love was infinite, if spring make it more.
But if this medicine, love, which cures all sorrow
With more, not only be no quintessence,
But mixed of all stuffs, paining soul, or sense,
10   And of the sun his working vigour borrow,
Love's not so pure, and abstract, as they use
To say, which have no mistress but their Muse,
But as all else, being elemented too,
Love sometimes would contemplate, sometimes do.

15   And yet not greater, but more eminent,
    Love by the spring is grown;
    As, in the firmament,
Stars by the sun are not enlarged, but shown,
Gentle love deeds, as blossoms on a bough,
20   From love's awakened root do bud out now.
If, as in water stirred more circles be
Produced by one, love such additions take,
Those like so many spheres, but one heaven make,
For, they are all concentric unto thee,
25   And though each spring do add to love new heat,
As princes do in times of action get
New taxes, and remit them not in peace,
No winter shall abate the spring's increase.

A Nocturnal upon S. Lucy's Day, being the shortest day

'Tis the year's midnight, and it is the day's,
Lucy's, who scarce seven hours herself unmasks,
    The sun is spent, and now his flasks
    Send forth light squibs, no constant rays;
5   The world's whole sap is sunk:
The general balm th' hydroptic earth hath drunk,
Whither, as to the bed's-feet, life is shrunk,
Dead and interred; yet all these seem to laugh,
Compared with me, who am their epitaph.

10 Study me then, you who shall lovers be
At the next world, that is, at the next spring:
    For I am every dead thing,
    In whom love wrought new alchemy.
      For his art did express
15 A quintessence even from nothingness,
From dull privations, and lean emptiness
He ruined me, and I am re-begot
Of absence, darkness, death; things which are not.

All others, from all things, draw all that's good,
20 Life, soul, form, spirit, whence they being have;
    I, by love's limbeck, am the grave
    Of all, that's nothing. Oft a flood
      Have we two wept, and so
Drowned the whole world, us two; oft did we grow
25 To be two chaoses, when we did show
Care to aught else; and often absences
Withdrew our souls, and made us carcases.

But I am by her death (which word wrongs her)
Of the first nothing, the elixir grown;
30   Were I a man, that I were one,
    I needs must know; I should prefer,
      If I were any beast,
Some ends, some means; yea plants, yea stones
    detest,
And love; all, all some properties invest;
35 If I an ordinary nothing were,
As shadow, a light, and body must be here.

But I am none; nor will my sun renew.
You lovers, for whose sake, the lesser sun
    At this time to the Goat is run
40   To fetch new lust, and give it you,
      Enjoy your summer all;
Since she enjoys her long night's festival,
Let me prepare towards her, and let me call
This hour her vigil, and her eve, since this
45 Both the year's, and the day's deep midnight is.

The Relic

When my grave is broke up again
Some second guest to entertain,
(For graves have learned that woman-head
To be to more than one a bed)
5   And he that digs it, spies
A bracelet of bright hair about the bone,
            Will he not let us alone,
And think that there a loving couple lies,
Who thought that this device might be some way
10   To make their souls, at the last busy day,
Meet at this grave, and make a little stay?
            If this fall in a time, or land,
                Where mis-devotion doth command,
                Then, he that digs us up, will bring
15   Us, to the Bishop, and the King,
                To make us relics; then
Thou shalt be a Mary Magdalen, and I
                A something else thereby;
All women shall adore us, and some men;
20   And since at such time, miracles are sought,
I would have that age by this paper taught
What miracles we harmless lovers wrought.

            First, we loved well and faithfully,
                Yet knew not what we loved, nor why,
25   Difference of sex no more we knew,
                Than our guardian angels do;
                Coming and going, we
Perchance might kiss, but not between those meals;
                Our hands ne'er touched the seals,
30   Which nature, injured by late law, sets free:
These miracles we did; but now alas,
All measure, and all language, I should pass,
Should I tell what a miracle she was.

Song

Go, and catch a falling star,
    Get with child a mandrake root,
Tell me, where all past years are,
    Or who cleft the Devil's foot,
5   Teach me to hear mermaids singing,
      Or to keep off envy's stinging,
        And find
        What wind
Serves to advance an honest mind.

10   If thou be'est born to strange sights,
      Things invisible to see,
Ride ten thousand days and nights,
    Till age snow white hairs on thee,
Thou, when thou return'st, wilt tell me
15   All strange wonders that befell thee,
        And swear
        No where
Lives a woman true, and fair.

If thou find'st one, let me know,
20   Such a pilgrimage were sweet,
Yet do not, I would not go,
    Though at next door we might meet,
Though she were true, when you met her,
And last, till you write your letter,
25   Yet she
        Will be
False, ere I come, to two, or three.

Song

Sweetest love, I do not go,
    For weariness of thee,
Nor in hope the world can show
    A fitter love for me;
5   But since that I
Must die at last, 'tis best,
To use my self in jest
    Thus by feigned deaths to die.

Yesternight the sun went hence,
10   And yet is here today,
He hath no desire nor sense,
    Nor half so short a way:
    Then fear not me,
But believe that I shall make
15   Speedier journeys, since I take
    More wings and spurs than he.

O how feeble is man's power,
    That if good fortune fall,
Cannot add another hour,
20   Nor a lost hour recall!
    But come bad chance,
And we join to it our strength,
And we teach it art and length,
    Itself o'er us to advance.

25 When thou sigh'st, thou sigh'st not wind,
    But sigh'st my soul away,
When thou weep'st, unkindly kind,
    My life's blood doth decay.

It cannot be
30 That thou lov'st me, as thou say'st,
If in thine my life thou waste,
Thou art the best of me.

Let not thy divining heart
Forethink me any ill,
35 Destiny may take thy part,
And may thy fears fulfil;
But think that we
Are but turned aside to sleep;
They who one another keep
40 Alive, ne'er parted be.

The Sun Rising

Busy old fool, unruly sun,
Why dost thou thus,
Through windows, and through curtains call on us?
Must to thy motions lovers' seasons run?
5 Saucy pedantic wretch, go chide
Late school-boys, and sour prentices,
Go tell court-huntsmen, that the King will ride,
Call country ants to harvest offices;
Love, all alike, no season knows, nor clime,
10 Nor hours, days, months, which are the rags of time.

Thy beams, so reverend, and strong
Why shouldst thou think?
I could eclipse and cloud them with a wink,
But that I would not lose her sight so long:
15 If her eyes have not blinded thine,

> Look, and tomorrow late, tell me,
>   Whether both th'Indias of spice and mine
>   Be where thou left'st them, or lie here with me.
> Ask for those kings whom thou saw'st yesterday,
> And thou shalt hear, All here in one bed lay.

>   She'is all states, and all princes, I,
>   Nothing else is.
> Princes do but play us; compared to this,
> All honour's mimic; all wealth alchemy.
>   Thou sun art half as happy as we,
>   In that the world's contracted thus;
>   Thine age asks ease, and since thy duties be
>   To warm the world, that's done in warming us.
> Shine here to us, and thou art everywhere;
> This bed thy centre is, these walls, thy sphere.

20

25

30

The Triple Fool

> I am two fools, I know,
> For loving, and for saying so
>   In whining poetry;
> But where's that wiseman, that would not be I,
>   If she would not deny?
> Then as th'earth's inward narrow crooked lanes
> Do purge sea water's fretful salt away,
>   I thought, if I could draw my pains
> Through rhyme's vexation, I should them allay.
>   Grief brought to numbers cannot be so fierce,
> For, he tames it, that fetters it in verse

5

10

But when I have done so,
Some man, his art and voice to show,
    Doth set and sing my pain,
15   And, by delighting many, frees again
      Grief, which verse did restrain.
To love and grief tribute of verse belongs,
But not of such as pleases when 'tis read,
    Both are increased by such songs:
20   For both their triumphs so are published,
And I, which was two fools, do so grow three;
Who are a little wise, the best fools be.

Twicknam Garden

Blasted with sighs, and surrounded with tears,
    Hither I come to seek the spring,
    And at mine eyes, and at mine ears,
Receive such balms, as else cure everything;
5   But O, self traitor, I do bring
The spider love, which transubstantiates all,
    And can convert manna to gall,
And that this place may thoroughly be thought
    True paradise, I have the serpent brought.

10 'Twere wholesomer for me, that winter did
    Benight the glory of this place,
    And that a grave frost did forbid
These trees to laugh, and mock me to my face;
    But that I may not this disgrace
15 Endure, nor yet leave loving, Love, let me
    Some senseless piece of this place be;
Make me a mandrake, so I may groan here,
    Or a stone fountain weeping out my year.

Hither with crystal vials, lovers come,
20   And take my tears, which are love's wine,
And try your mistress' tears at home,
For all are false, that taste not just like mine;
      Alas, hearts do not in eyes shine,
Nor can you more judge woman's thoughts by tears,
25   Than by her shadow, what she wears.
O perverse sex, where none is true but she,
      Who's therefore true, because her truth kills me.

The Undertaking

I have done one braver thing
      Than all the Worthies did,
And yet a braver thence doth spring,
      Which is, to keep that hid.

5   It were but madness now t'impart
      The skill of specular stone,
When he which can have learned the art
      To cut it, can find none.

So, if I now should utter this,
10   Others (because no more
Such stuff to work upon, there is,)
      Would love but as before.

But he who loveliness within
      Hath found, all outward loathes,
15   For he who colour loves, and skin,
      Loves but their oldest clothes.

If, as I have, you also do
    Virtue attired in woman see,
And dare love that, and say so too,
20   And forget the He and She;

And if this love, though placed so,
    From profane men you hide,
Which will no faith on this bestow,
    Or, if they do, deride:

25 Then you have done a braver thing
    Than all the Worthies did,
And a braver thence will spring,
    Which is, to keep that hid.

A Valediction: forbidding Mourning

As virtuous men pass mildly away,
    And whisper to their souls, to go,
Whilst some of their sad friends do say,
    The breath goes now, and some say, no:

5 So let us melt, and make no noise,
    No tear-floods, nor sigh-tempests move,
'Twere profanation of our joys
    To tell the laity our love.

Moving of th' earth brings harms and fears,
10   Men reckon what it did and meant,
But trepidation of the spheres,
    Though greater far, is innocent.

Dull sublunary lovers' love
   (Whose soul is sense) cannot admit
15 Absence, because it doth remove
   Those things which elemented it.

But we by a love, so much refined,
   That our selves know not what it is,
Inter-assured of the mind,
20   Care less, eyes, lips, and hands to miss.

Our two souls therefore, which are one,
   Though I must go, endure not yet
A breach, but an expansion,
   Like gold to aery thinness beat.

25 If they be two, they are two so
   As stiff twin compasses are two,
Thy soul the fixed foot, makes no show
   To move, but doth, if th'other do.

And though it in the centre sit,
30   Yet when the other far doth roam,
It leans, and hearkens after it,
   And grows erect, as that comes home.

Such wilt thou be to me, who must
   Like th' other foot, obliquely run;
35 Thy firmness makes my circle just,
   And makes me end, where I begun.

A Valediction: of Weeping

       Let me pour forth
My tears before thy face, whilst I stay here,
For thy face coins them, and thy stamp they bear,
And by this mintage they are something worth,
5   For thus they be
       Pregnant of thee;
Fruits of much grief they are, emblems of more,
When a tear falls, that thou falls which it bore,
So thou and I are nothing then, when on a divers shore.

10   On a round ball
A workman that hath copies by, can lay
An Europe, Afric, and an Asia,
And quickly make that, which was nothing, all,
       So doth each tear,
15   Which thee doth wear,
A globe, yea world by that impression grow,
Till thy tears mixed with mine do overflow
This world, by waters sent from thee, my heaven dissolved so

       O more than moon,
20 Draw not up seas to drown me in thy sphere,
Weep me not dead, in thine arms, but forbear
To teach the sea, what it may do too soon;
       Let not the wind
       Example find,
25 To do me more harm, than it purposeth;
Since thou and I sigh one another's breath,
Whoe'er sighs most, is cruellest, and hastes the other's death.

Woman's Constancy

Now thou hast loved me one whole day,
Tomorrow when thou leav'st, what wilt thou say?
Wilt thou then antedate some new made vow?
        Or say that now
5   We are not just those persons, which we were?
Or, that oaths made in reverential fear
Of Love, and his wrath, any may forswear?
Or, as true deaths, true marriages untie,
So lovers' contracts, images of those,
10   Bind but till sleep, death's image, them unloose?
        Or, your own end to justify,
For having purposed change, and falsehood, you
Can have no way but falsehood to be true?
Vain lunatic, against these 'scapes I could
15   Dispute, and conquer, if I would,
            Which I abstain to do,
For by tomorrow, I may think so too.

Elegies

Elegy 4: The Perfume

Once, and but once found in thy company,
All thy supposed escapes are laid on me;
And as a thief at bar, is questioned there
By all the men, that have been robbed that year,
5   So am I, (by this traitorous means surprised)
By thy hydroptic father catechized.
Though he had wont to search with glazed eyes,
As though he came to kill a cockatrice,
Though he have oft sworn, that he would remove
10   Thy beauty's beauty, and food of our love,
Hope of his goods, if I with thee were seen,
Yet close and secret, as our souls, we have been.
Though thy immortal mother which doth lie
Still buried in her bed, yet will not die,
15   Takes this advantage to sleep out day-light,
And watch thy entries, and returns all night,
And, when she takes thy hand, and would seem kind,
Doth search what rings, and armlets she can find,
And kissing notes the colour of thy face,
20   And fearing less thou art swoll'n, doth thee embrace;
To try if thou long, doth name strange meats,
And notes thy paleness, blushing, sighs, and sweats;
And politicly will to thee confess
The sins of her own youth's rank lustiness;
25   Yet love these sorceries did remove, and move
Thee to gull thine own mother for my love.
Thy little brethren, which like faery sprites
Oft skipped into our chamber, those sweet nights,
And kissed, and ingled on thy father's knee,
30   Were bribed next day, to tell what they did see.

The grim eight-foot-high iron-bound serving-man,
That oft names God in oaths, and only then,
He that to bar the first gate, doth as wide
As the great Rhodian Colossus stride,

35 Which, if in hell no other pains there were,
Makes me fear hell, because he must be there:
Though by thy father he were hired to this,
Could never witness any touch or kiss.
But Oh, too common ill, I brought with me

40 That, which betrayed me to mine enemy:
A loud perfume, which at my entrance cried
Even at thy father's nose, so we were spied.
When, like a tyrant king, that in his bed
Smelt gunpowder, the pale wretch shivered.

45 Had it been some bad smell, he would have thought
That his own feet, or breath, that smell had wrought.
But as we in our isle imprisoned,
Where cattle only, and diverse dogs are bred,
The precious unicorns, strange monsters call,

50 So thought he good, strange, that had none at all.
I taught my silks, their whistling to forbear,
Even my oppressed shoes, dumb and speechless were,
Only, thou bitter sweet, whom I had laid
Next me, me traitorously hast betrayed,

55 And unsuspected hast invisibly
At once fled unto him, and stayed with me.
Base excrement of earth, which dost confound
Sense, from distinguishing the sick from sound;
By thee the silly amorous sucks his death

60 By drawing in a leprous harlot's breath;
By thee, the greatest stain to man's estate
Falls on us, to be called effeminate;
Though you be much loved in the prince's hall,
There, things that seem, exceed substantial.

65 Gods, when ye fumed on altars, were pleased well,

53

Because you were burnt, not that they liked your
    smell;
You are loathsome all, being taken simply alone,
Shall we love ill things joined, and hate each one?
If you were good, your good doth soon decay;
70 And you are rare, that takes the good away.
All my perfumes, I give most willingly
To embalm thy father's corse; What? will he die?

Elegy 5: His Picture

Here take my picture, though I bid farewell;
Thine, in my heart, where my soul dwells, shall
    dwell.
'Tis like me now, but I dead, 'twill be more
When we are shadows both, than 'twas before.
5 When weather-beaten I come back; my hand,
Perhaps with rude oars torn, or sun-beams tanned,
My face and breast of haircloth, and my head
With care's rash sudden hoariness o'erspread,
My body a sack of bones, broken within,
10 And powder's blue stains scattered on my skin;
If rival fools tax thee to have loved a man,
So foul, and coarse, as oh, I may seem then,
This shall say what I was: and thou shalt say,
Do his hurts reach me? doth my worth decay?
15 Or do they reach his judging mind, that he
Should now love less, what he did love to see?
That which in him was fair and delicate,
Was but the milk, which in love's childish state
Did nurse it: who now is grown strong enough
20 To feed on that, which to disused tastes seems tough.

Elegy 16: On his Mistress

By our first strange and fatal interview,
By all desires which thereof did ensue,
By our long starving hopes, by that remorse
Which my words' masculine persuasive force
5   Begot in thee, and by the memory
Of hurts, which spies and rivals threatened me,
I calmly beg: but by thy father's wrath,
By all pains, which want and divorcement hath,
I conjure thee; and all the oaths which I
10   And thou have sworn to seal joint constancy,
Here I unswear, and overswear them thus,
Thou shalt not love by ways so dangerous.
Temper, O fair love, love's impetuous rage,
Be my true mistress still, not my feigned page;
15   I'll go, and, by thy kind leave, leave behind
Thee, only worthy to nurse in my mind
Thirst to come back; oh, if thou die before,
From other lands my soul towards thee shall soar,
Thy (else almighty) beauty cannot move
20   Rage from the seas, nor thy love teach them love,
Nor tame wild Boreas' harshness; thou hast read
How roughly he in pieces shivered
Fair Orithea, whom he swore he loved.
Fall ill or good, 'tis madness to have proved
25   Dangers unurged; feed on this flattery,
That absent lovers one in th' other be.
Dissemble nothing, not a boy, nor change
Thy body's habit, nor mind's; be not strange
To thy self only; all will spy in thy face
30   A blushing womanly discovering grace;
Richly clothed apes, are called apes, and as soon

Eclipsed as bright we call the moon the moon.
Men of France, changeable chameleons,
Spitals of diseases, shops of fashions,
35 Love's fuellers, and the rightest company
Of players, which upon the world's stage be,
Will quickly know thee, and know thee; and alas
Th' indifferent Italian, as we pass
His warm land, well content to think thee page,
40 Will hunt thee with such lust, and hideous rage,
As Lot's fair guests were vexed. But none of these
Nor spongy hydroptic Dutch shall thee displease,
If thou stay here. Oh stay here, for, for thee
England is only a worthy gallery,
45 To walk in expectation, till from thence
Our greatest King call thee to his presence.
When I am gone, dream me some happiness,
Nor let thy looks our long-hid love confess,
Nor praise, nor dispraise me, nor bless nor curse
50 Openly love's force, nor in bed fright thy nurse
With midnight's startings, crying out, 'Oh, oh
Nurse, O my love is slain, I saw him go
O'er the white Alps alone; I saw him, I,
Assailed, fight, taken, stabbed, bleed, fall, and die.'
55 Augur me better chance, except dread Jove
Think it enough for me to have had thy love.

Elegy 19: To his Mistress Going to Bed

Come, Madam, come, all rest my powers defy,
Until I labour, I in labour lie.
The foe oft-times having the foe in sight,

Is tried with standing though he never fight.
5   Off with that girdle, like heaven's zone glistering,
But a far fairer world encompassing.
Unpin that spangled breastplate which you wear,
That th' eyes of busy fools may be stopped there.
Unlace yourself, for that harmonious chime
10   Tells me from you, that now 'tis your bed time.
Off with that happy busk, which I envy,
That still can be, and still can stand so nigh.
Your gown going off, such beauteous state reveals,
As when from flowery meads th' hill's shadow steals.
15   Off with that wiry coronet and show
The hairy diadem which on you doth grow;
Now off with those shoes, and then safely tread
In this love's hallowed temple, this soft bed.
In such white robes heaven's angels used to be
20   Received by men; thou angel bring'st with thee
A heaven like Mahomet's paradise; and though
Ill spirits walk in white, we easily know
By this these angels from an evil sprite,
Those set our hairs, but these our flesh upright.
25   License my roving hands, and let them go
Before, behind, between, above, below.
O my America, my new found land,
My kingdom, safeliest when with one man manned,
My mine of precious stones, my empery,
30   How blessed am I in this discovering thee!
To enter in these bonds, is to be free;
Then where my hand is set, my seal shall be.
        Full nakedness, all joys are due to thee.
As souls unbodied, bodies unclothed must be,
35   To taste whole joys. Gems which you women use
Are like Atlanta's balls, cast in men's views,
That when a fool's eye lighteth on a gem,

His earthly soul may covet theirs, not them.
Like pictures, or like books' gay coverings made
40 For laymen, are all women thus arrayed;
Themselves are mystic books, which only we
Whom their imputed grace will dignify
Must see revealed. Then since I may know,
As liberally, as to a midwife, show
45 Thyself: cast all, yea, this white linen hence,
Here is no penance, much less innocence.
      To teach thee, I am naked first, why then
What needst thou have more covering than a man.

Religious Poems

Holy sonnets

6

This is my play's last scene, here heavens appoint
My pilgrimage's last mile; and my race
Idly, yet quickly run, hath this last pace,
My span's last inch, my minute's latest point,
5   And gluttonous death, will instantly unjoint
My body, and soul, and I shall sleep a space,
But my'ever-waking part shall see that face,
Whose fear already shakes my every joint:
Then, as my soul, to heaven her first seat, takes flight,
10   And earth-born body, in the earth shall dwell,
So, fall my sins, that all may have their right,
To where they are bred, and would press me, to hell.
Impute me righteous, thus purged of evil,
For thus I leave the world, the flesh, and devil.

7

At the round earth's imagined corners, blow
Your trumpets, angels, and arise, arise
From death, you numberless infinities
Of souls, and to your scattered bodies go,
5   All whom the flood did, and fire shall o'erthrow,
All whom war, dearth, age, agues, tyrannies,
Despair, law, chance, hath slain, and you whose eyes,
Shall behold God, and never taste death's woe.
But let them sleep, Lord, and me mourn a space,
10   For, if above all these, my sins abound,
'Tis late to ask abundance of thy grace,
When we are there; here on this lowly ground,
Teach me how to repent; for that's as good
As if thou hadst sealed my pardon, with thy blood.

10

Death be not proud, though some have called thee
Mighty and dreadful, for, thou art not so,
For, those, whom thou think'st, thou dost
    overthrow,
Die not, poor death, nor yet canst thou kill me;
5   From rest and sleep, which but thy pictures be,
Much pleasure, then from thee, much more must
    flow,
And soonest our best men with thee do go,
Rest of their bones, and soul's delivery.
Thou art slave to fate, chance, kings, and desperate
    men,
10   And dost with poison, war, and sickness dwell,
And poppy, or charms can make us sleep as well,
And better than thy stroke; why swell'st thou then?
One short sleep past, we wake eternally,
And death shall be no more, Death thou shalt die.

13

What if this present were the world's last night?
Mark in my heart, O soul, where thou dost dwell,
The picture of Christ crucified, and tell
Whether that countenance can thee affright,
5   Tears in his eyes quench the amazing light,
Blood fills his frowns, which from his pierced head
    fell,
And can that tongue adjudge thee unto hell,
Which prayed forgiveness for his foes' fierce spite?
No, no; but as in my idolatry
10   I said to all my profane mistresses,
Beauty, of pity, foulness only is
A sign of rigour: so I say to thee,
To wicked spirits are horrid shapes assigned,
This beauteous form assures a piteous mind.

14

Batter my heart, three-personed God; for, you
As yet but knock, breathe, shine, and seek to mend;
That I may rise, and stand, o'erthrow me, and bend
Your force, to break, blow, burn, and make me new.
5   I, like an usurped town, to another due,
Labour to admit you, but oh, to no end,
Reason your viceroy in me, me should defend,
But is captived, and proves weak or untrue,
Yet dearly'I love you, and would be loved fain,
10   But am betrothed unto your enemy,
Divorce me, untie, or break that knot again,
Take me to you, imprison me, for I
Except you enthral me, never shall be free,
Nor ever chaste, except you ravish me.

17

Since she whom I loved hath paid her last debt
To nature, and to hers, and my good is dead,
And her soul early into heaven ravished,
Wholly in heavenly things my mind is set.
5   Here the admiring her my mind did whet
To seek thee God; so streams do show the head,
But though I have found thee, and thou my thirst
    hast fed,
A holy thirsty dropsy melts me yet.
But why should I beg more love, when as thou
10   Dost woo my soul for hers; offering all thine:
And dost not only fear lest I allow
My love to saints and angels, things divine,
But in thy tender jealousy dost doubt
Lest the world, flesh, yea Devil put thee out.

19

Oh, to vex me, contraries meet in one:
Inconstancy unnaturally hath begot
A constant habit; that when I would not
I change in vows, and in devotion.
5   As humorous is my contrition
As my profane love, and as soon forgot:
As riddlingly distempered, cold and hot,
As praying, as mute; as infinite, as none.
I durst not view heaven yesterday; and today
10   In prayers, and flattering speeches I court God:
Tomorrow I quake with true fear of his rod.
So my devout fits come and go away
Like a fantastic ague: save that here
Those are my best days, when I shake with fear.

Good Friday, 1613. Riding Westward

Let man's soul be a sphere, and then, in this,
The intelligence that moves, devotion is,
And as the other spheres, by being grown
Subject to foreign motions, lose their own,
5   And being by others hurried every day,
Scarce in a year their natural form obey:
Pleasure or business, so, our souls admit
For their first mover, and are whirled by it.
Hence is't, that I am carried towards the west
10   This day, when my soul's form bends toward the east.
There I should see a sun, by rising set,
And by that setting endless day beget;
But that Christ on this Cross, did rise and fall,

Sin had eternally benighted all.
15   Yet dare I'almost be glad, I do not see
That spectacle of too much weight for me.
Who sees God's face, that is self life, must die;
What a death were it then to see God die?
It made his own lieutenant Nature shrink,
20   It made his footstool crack, and the sun wink.
Could I behold those hands which span the poles,
And turn all spheres at once, pierced with those holes?
Could I behold that endless height which is
Zenith to us, and to'our antipodes,
25   Humbled below us? or that blood which is
The seat of all our souls, if not of his,
Made dirt of dust, or that flesh which was worn,
By God, for his apparel, ragged, and torn?
If on these things I durst not look, durst I
30   Upon his miserable mother cast mine eye,
Who was God's partner here, and furnished thus
Half of that sacrifice, which ransomed us?
Though these things, as I ride, be from mine eye,
They are present yet unto my memory,
35   For that looks towards them; and thou look'st
           towards me,
O Saviour, as thou hang'st upon the tree;
I turn my back to thee, but to receive
Corrections, till thy mercies bid thee leave.
O think me worth thine anger, punish me,
40   Burn off my rusts, and my deformity,
Restore thine image, so much, by thy grace,
That thou mayst know me, and I'll turn my face.

A Hymn to Christ, at the Author's last going into Germany

In what torn ship soever I embark,
That ship shall be my emblem of thy ark;
What sea soever swallow me, that flood
Shall be to me an emblem of thy blood;
5   Though thou with clouds of anger do disguise
Thy face; yet through that mask I know those eyes,
      Which, though they turn away sometimes,
        They never will despise.

I sacrifice this Island unto thee,
10   And all whom I loved there, and who loved me;
When I have put our seas twixt them and me,
Put thou thy sea betwixt my sins and thee.
As the tree's sap doth seek the root below
In winter, in my winter now I go,
15   Where none but thee, th' eternal root
      Of true love I may know.

Nor thou nor thy religion dost control,
The amorousness of an harmonious soul,
But thou wouldst have that love thyself: as thou
20   Art jealous, Lord, so I am jealous now,
Thou lov'st not, till from loving more, thou free
My soul; who ever gives, takes liberty:
      O, if thou car'st not whom I love
        Alas, thou lov'st not me.

25 Seal then this bill of my divorce to all,
    On whom those fainter beams of love did fall;
    Marry those loves, which in youth scattered be
    On fame, wit, hopes (false mistresses) to thee.
    Churches are best for prayer, that have least light:
30 To see God only, I go out of sight:
        And to 'scape stormy days, I choose
        An everlasting night.

Hymn to God my God,
in my Sickness

Since I am coming to that holy room,
    Where, with thy choir of saints for evermore,
I shall be made thy music; as I come
    I tune the instrument here at the door,
5   And what I must do then, think here before.

Whilst my physicians by their love are grown
    Cosmographers, and I their map, who lie
Flat on this bed, that by them may be shown
    That this is my south-west discovery
10 *Per fretum febris*, by these straits to die,

I joy, that in these straits, I see my west;
    For, though their currents yield return to none,
What shall my west hurt me? As west and east
    In all flat maps (and I am one) are one,
15   So death doth touch the resurrection.

Is the Pacific Sea my home? Or are
    The eastern riches? Is Jerusalem?
Anyan, and Magellan, and Gibraltar,
    All straits, and none but straits, are ways to them,
20   Whether where Japhet dwelt, or Cham, or Shem.

We think that Paradise and Calvary,
    Christ's Cross, and Adam's tree, stood in one
        place;
Look Lord, and find both Adams met in me;
    As the first Adam's sweat surrounds my face,
25   May the last Adam's blood my soul embrace.

So, in his purple wrapped receive me Lord,
    By these his thorns give me his other crown;
And as to others' souls I preached thy word,
    Be this my text, my sermon to mine own,
30   Therefore that he may raise the Lord throws down.

A Hymn to God the Father

I
Wilt thou forgive that sin where I begun,
    Which was my sin, though it were done before?
Wilt thou forgive that sin, through which I run,
    And do run still: though still I do deplore?
5   When thou hast done, thou hast not done,
        For, I have more.

II
Wilt thou forgive that sin which I have won
    Others to sin? and, made my sin their door?
Wilt thou forgive that sin which I did shun
10   A year, or two: but wallowed in, a score?
      When thou hast done, thou hast not done,
        For I have more.

III
I have a sin of fear, that when I have spun
    My last thread, I shall perish on the shore;
15 But swear by thy self, that at my death thy son
    Shall shine as he shines now, and heretofore;
      And, having done that, thou hast done,
        I fear no more.

Notes

Air and Angels

In language as delicately insubstantial as its subject matter, Donne meditates on souls, light, love, a shapeless flame and angels. The music of its cadences and textures is appropriately airy and refined. The argument emerges so easily out of the varied and, in some cases, surprising imagery, the reader is carried to the conclusion (by no means an uncontroversial one) with a persuasive naturalness. For a discussion of the form of the poem, see Interpretations, p. 166.

The argument of the poem is elusive. Those who wish to follow it closely should read the discussions in Helen Gardner's *The Business of Criticism* and Theodore Redpath's summary in his edition of *The Songs and Sonnets of John Donne*, 1956.

Title It was a problem for medieval theology as to how angels, which are pure spirit, can become visible. Donne depends on the idea that they form bodies out of the air, because the air, while not as pure in substance as angels, is the purest of all the elements.

1 **Twice or thrice** Here, and throughout the poem, the reader should attend to the rhymes, repetitions of sounds and textures to appreciate the poem's sound world. Perhaps the verbal music is the enactment of the poem's interest in purity of substances.

2 **Before I knew** the same idea is present in *The Good Morrow* (6–7).

3 **shapeless flame** See Interpretations, p. 158.

4–5 See Interpretations, p. 158.

4 **affect** influence.
    worshipped adored and honoured. In contemporary love poetry, a beloved was an object of devotion and worship.

5 **still** on every occasion.

6 **lovely glorious nothing** listen to the note of wonder that runs through the poem.

7–8 The soul needs a body through which it can act. Donne is reversing Platonism. Plato taught that we should search for the Ideal Forms rather than concentrate on this or that particular object. Donne, however, says he has found the concrete embodiment of the Ideal Form of woman. See Context, p. 13 and Interpretations, p. 140.

9 **subtle**   a word concerned with refined and rarefied substances. In lines 23–4 angels take bodies of air, because it is the most pure and subtle of material substances.

10 **take a body too**   Platonism looks through bodies to Ideal Forms; Donne says that love must find a form – the flesh and blood of a human body – that can be the object of its loving.

11–12 The image is of the lover asking love what kind of a person his hitherto only glimpsed beloved is. Do you find the touch of courtesy – the lover asking a favour of love – appropriate?

13 **assume**   at least two ideas are present here. To assume is to take, in the sense that a soul takes a body in order to express itself. The word also means to be taken up into heaven. Perhaps the point is that heaven for the poet is to see the woman, who embodies all that he has ever longed for.
allow   to recognize and accept as true.

14 **lip, eye, and brow**   The reversal of Platonism (see Notes on 7–8 and 10 and Interpretations, p. 141) will only convince the reader if these lines express the wonder of discovery. See also A Valediction: forbidding Mourning (20).

15 **ballast**   weights carried in a ship so it can sail more steadily (16) and avoid capsizing. Does anything earlier in the poem prepare us for this surprising image?

17 **wares**   goods carried by a ship.

18 **pinnace**   a swift, light ship, so one that might easily be overloaded (*overfraught*). See Interpretations, p. 164.

19–20 This probably means: even every single one of your hairs overwhelms me. Is this one of the most wondering and loving lines in the entire poem?

20 **fitter**   more appropriate. This word introduces the final stage of the argument. Try to trace the entire movement of the argument in terms of the implicit images of reaching down for a body and reaching up for a refined love.

22 **Extreme, and scatt'ring bright**   Is this a good description of Donne's poems? See Interpretations, p. 139.

inhere   remain united with.
23–4 See Title note about how angels make themselves visible.
  25 Donne argues that his love will be the Intelligence that guides
      and moves the sphere of a planet or the sun. See Context, p. 7
      and *The Ecstasy* (51–2).
25–8 Is it possible to avoid the implication that male love is active
      and female love passive? If it is not, might some find the close
      of the poem disappointing?

The Anniversary

Think about how the buoyancy and triumph of the poem's
rhythms enforce two of its themes: the superiority of lovers over
common humanity and the relationship between love and time.
Is the second verse a problem? Do you find it disappointingly flat
after the exhilarating opening, or are you impressed because the
playful attitude to time has given way to a serious recognition of
the inevitability of death? See Interpretations, pp. 146-8.

   1 **favourites**   courtiers who are favoured by the King. Might this
      implicit dismissal of the court mean that it is less satisfying
      than the world of mutual love, or can it be that the poet is
      creating a compensatory world of mutual love because the
      court has rejected him? See also *The Canonization* and *The Sun
      Rising* and Context, p. 14.
   2 **honours... wits**   *honours* are either judges or privileges; *wits* are
      intellectuals.
7–10 See Interpretations, pp. 158-9.
  7–8 These lines contrast the triumphant close of the poem, in
      which love is numbered in years (29–30). What might this
      interesting tension show us about the movement of Donne's
      mind and the experience of being in love?
   9 **Running... runs**   think about how the grammatical difference
      between the participle *running* and the verb *runs* makes a
      distinction between permanence and change.
  10 **first, last, everlasting day**   the first day of creation, the day of
      judgement and eternity.

11 **corse**   corpse.

12 **divorce**   are the lovers married? As the word *divorce* only
applies to those who have been married, we may assume so. But
if they are married, why would they be buried in two graves?
Perhaps we have to consider the grisly idea that if they had
shared one grave, their souls would have been reluctant to leave
their decaying corpses on the day of judgement.

15–20 These lines, as is often the case in Donne, are divided between
his wonder at the body (think about the lingering regret of
leaving *these eyes, and ears*, line 15) and the hope, caught in an
unexpected rhyme, of a *love increased there above* (19). In the light
of the metaphors associated with occupation – an owner *dwells*
but lodgers are *inmates* – think about the relationship between
the soul, the body and the grave. See Interpretations, p. 141.

18 **prove**   experience will show it to be true.

21 **throughly**   thoroughly, completely.

23 **Here upon earth** ′ do these words show what chiefly interests
the poet, and if so, what is to be made of the second stanza
with its vision of a love perfected in heaven?

25 **Who is so safe as we?**   does this rhetorical question work
because the reader sees that lovers are significantly different
from kings, or is it bravado trying to counter a real doubt that
they might not be safe? A similar question can be asked of
Treason (26). See Interpretations, p. 150.

27 **True and false fears**   what is to be feared – time or
unfaithfulness? It is also problematic as to which is the *true* and
which the *false* fear.

29 **Years and years unto years**   do the rhythms of this line
emphasize the glorious character of their noble reign in the
kingdom of love, or is there a hint of the grinding
repetitiveness of passing years?

30 **threescore**   since the span of life is usually said to be
threescore years and ten (seventy years), is the idea that the
lovers are so superior that their reign lasts longer? If so, is the
image of aged lovers disconcerting?

The Apparition

One of the teasing things about this dramatic poem is its tone: is it one of vitriolic rage or that of someone who relishes the grotesque comedy of a ghost succeeding in reaching the woman's bed, when the living man did not? The language of crime, guilt and repentance is likewise ambivalent (see Interpretations, p. x). The problem of tone also touches on the issue of how the poem might be performed: the reader will have to decide whether words such as *When* (1), *Then* (4) (6) and *since my love is spent* (15) should be read with anger or amused playfulness. See Interpretations, p. 143 and p. 145.

3 **solicitation**   the act of earnestly requesting or begging something.
5 **vestal**   vestal virgins were Roman women who lived chaste lives of dedicated religious service.
6 **taper**   candle.
10 **shrink**   does this mean more than the act of a tired lover recoiling from a sexually-demanding woman?
11 **aspen**   a type of poplar noted for the way its leaves tremble in the wind.
12 **quicksilver**   there may be a hint of poison here, as mercury vapour was known to be poisonous.
13 **A verier ghost**   even more of a ghost.
14 See Interpretations, p. 162.
15 **and since my love is spent**   this seems to contradict the opening line, where the poet envisages himself as dead from unrequited love. Is he really in love and hoping that these words will make her submit to him? Is his desire for revenge stronger than his love? Is he pretending to love so that she might feel guilty? Whatever the answer, the inconsistency between (1) and (15) underlines the ambivalence of the poet's attitude. There may be a suggestion of ejaculation in *spent*.

Notes

Break of Day

The voice of the poem is a woman (see Interpretations, p. 141).
Readers may wonder whether Donne has deliberately fashioned
a female voice or whether it is argument rather than gender that
interests him. Perhaps the pleading (even beguiling) tone is
consciously female. But then, readers might think that the
reasons the woman so cleverly urges make it not unlike *Woman's
Constancy*. Perhaps *Break of Day* does not have the dismissive
gusto of *Woman's Constancy*, but it shares with that poem a
delight in agile reasoning. See Interpretations, p. 142.

Title Women requesting the lover not to leave after a night together
is a theme going back to late medieval love poetry. Juliet's plea
to Romeo shows how strong the tradition was.

1 **'Tis true** as in the case of other Donne poems (*The Flea*, for
instance), this is presented as a conversation in which the reader
only hears one voice.

3–4 Do we enjoy her frank admission that they did not go to bed
because it was night?

7 **light** in literature, light is sometimes used to expose
wickedness. Is there a touch of guilt here?

12 **that had them** the meaning seems to be that in having her, the
lover now has the honour that was once hers. What is her
attitude? Is she now dependent upon him, or is there an
attractive boldness in her acceptance that, in the traditional
sense, her honour was lost with her virginity?

16 **busied man** do we see that he is making excuses to leave her
or that she is cleverly portraying him as a small-minded man,
preoccupied with trivial matters?

18 **married man** is there a suggestion here that the man is
adulterous?

The Canonization

This could be called a retirement poem, in that the poet vehemently scorns the public world and opts, instead, for an intimate world of love. (Some scholars have speculated that Donne wrote it in the early years of his marriage, when, due largely to the hostility of his father-in-law, his future was in question.) This might account for how the poet both recognizes the uncertainty of the world yet considers its dangers with amused detachment. But if it is about retirement, why does the poem close with the lovers as objects of adoration by *all* (35)? Two further questions are whether, for all its religious language, the poem actually celebrates an entirely earthly love, and whether the poem's changing emotional life matters more than the poem's argument.

Title   The central idea of the poem is that the lovers have been canonized – declared to be saints – *for love* (36). This could mean that their love has a mysterious and unearthly quality, or that they have been martyred by those who have excluded them from the public world, or that their loving has been so vigorous they have become martyrs by wearing themselves out. See Interpretations, p. 150.

1   This colloquial outburst (and many other lines) are remarkable for the abruptness of their speech rhythms. A reading of the poem might help you to discover how its emotional and intellectual life is dependent upon these speech rhythms and, also, which are the poem's most crucial words.

2   **palsy... gout** *palsy* is trembling or paralysis; *gout* a disease affecting the joints, commonly associated with old men.

4–9   The emotional cross-currents of these lines might make us wonder about the poet's attitudes. Does he scornfully dismiss the disturber and the public world with the fierce conviction of a moralist or are there elements of fascination, perhaps even of envy, in the way he quickly scans such worldly concerns as commerce, learning, society and the court? A clue might be found by considering the force of the carefully placed verbs – *Take... get... Observe... Contemplate*: do they suggest purposeful

Notes

activity that is the envy of the poet, or is there something comically mechanical about their frenetic busyness?

6 **Honour... Grace**   a Lord and a Bishop or Archbishop.

7 **stamped face**   a coin bearing the king's head. (The language of economics is a recurring feature of the poem.)

10–18 What is the poet's attitude in this stanza? If there is scorn in his voice, is it still directed at the disturber, or is his real target those Petrarchan love poets who write of lovers' tears drowning the world or their sighs creating storms? (See Context, p. 15.) Alternatively, is the poet actually revelling in poetic exaggeration?

20 **fly**   a moth irresistibly attracted to a candle (*taper*).

21 **die**   here, as elsewhere in Donne, there may be a play upon *die*, meaning the loss of sexual power after consummation. The traditional idea that sexual intercourse shortens life may also be present.

22–7 The *eagle* is emblematic of masculine sexual initiative and the *dove* of female gentleness and sexual compliance. The *phoenix* is a mythical bird which every thousand years rejuvenates itself by being consumed in flames and rising renewed from its ashes. It was thus emblematic of the resurrection, though here the renewal of sexual power – *we die and rise* (26) – is prominent.

27 **Mysterious**   does the poem makes us feel that their love is mysterious in the sense of being special and holy? In the following stanzas religious language enforces associations of other-worldliness, but does the impression that their love is only sexual athleticism still persist? Line 28 raises this problem acutely: if *die* is literal, then the religious language which follows might convince us that their love is truly mysterious, but what if the sexual connotations of *die* are acknowledged?

32 **sonnets... rooms**   *sonnets* here probably means love lyrics. In Italian, stanza, a unit of verse, means a room. This wordplay raises the question of whether at this point the speaker (or Donne?) is as interested in the nature of writing as in the nature of love. Consider, for instance, the force of *legend* (an inscription), *verse* and *hymns*.

38 **hermitage**   how far should this conceit be pressed? Does it signify their deep mutual understanding or does it point to their sexual union?

76

39 See Interpretations, p. 148.
40–3 Do these lines mean that the lovers find in each other the essence of all that is valuable in the wider world, or that they possess each other so intensely that they seem to own everything?
44 See Context, p. 13.
45 **pattern** this may recall the Platonic idea (see Context, p. 13) of Ideal Forms towards which the earthly world aspires. This raises the issue of whether the poet wants an earthly or a heavenly love.

The Damp

The voice of the poet is firm and purposeful, yet judging the poem's tone and attitude is no easy matter. Is, for instance, the opening scene of the autopsy anything more than grotesque comedy? And what is to be made of the frank language of the closing stanza with its playing on the sexual connotations of *die* (21) (see Interpretations, p. 146). Is this an honest recognition of desire or a reductive picture of the relations between men and women? (See Context, pp. 5-6.) For tone and viewpoint see Interpretations, p. 145.

Title A *damp* is either a noxious fume or a moist, heavy air which depresses or even poisons those who breathe it.
1 **When I am dead** the abrupt monosyllabic wording is echoed by other lines; for instance, *but if you dare be brave* (9). Does the monosyllabic thrust suggest annoyance, frustration, the desire to dominate or purposefulness?
3 **cut up** a very emphatic stress falls upon these words. The words might bring out the oddity the poet feels at being an anatomical object or show hostility to the mistress.
4 **your picture in my heart** is the tone here one of surprise similar to *The Relic* or perhaps grudging flattery, implying that her picture in his heart is only to be expected? (See Context, p. 15.)

7 **prefer** promote.

10 **pleasure** the pleasure she takes in her conquests makes her a conventional cruel mistress, delighting in the sufferings she causes. It is, however, important to ask whether, in the poem as a whole, the poet thinks of his pleasure.

11 **enormous giant** at this point the poem touches on the twilight world of medieval romance with its *enchantress* (12) and *witches* (18). This language works allegorically; the *enormous giant* is *your Disdain*. The implication might be that her morality is as out-dated as medieval literary forms. It may also be that Donne the poet enjoys working in another mode.

13 **Goth and Vandal** the Goths and Vandals were Germanic tribes whose frequent and violent attacks brought about the downfall of the Roman Empire. Their names are traditionally associated with destruction.

16 **Kill... die** see general note and *The Canonization* (21).

20–4 Do you recoil from the masculine assertiveness of these lines, particularly the demand that the woman exercise her *passive valour* (23)? Another possibility is that, as women were thought of as passive in the sexual act, *valour* (a term from medieval romance) might be a recognition of her power. But see note on line 11.

24 The idea is that in sexual encounters women can perform far longer than men.

The Dream

This poem's chief characteristic is the delight the poet takes in his extravagant wit. In the first eight lines, pleasure in his mistress leads him to that branch of philosophy called epistemology – the nature of and the methods used in gaining knowledge. His *dream* is a *theme/For reason* not *for phantasy* (3–4), and she is such as to *make dreams truths* (8). Plato is not very far away here (see Context, pp. 12-13). Later, there is a witty use of religious language. He implies that her knowledge is *beyond an angel's art* (16), thereby equating it with God's knowledge. Also bold is his use of *cam'st* (18), *rising* (22) and *goest to come* (29) as descriptive of the movements of the woman and the pattern of Christ's birth, rising from the dead, ascension into heaven and return at the end of time. Perhaps this is a poem that should just be enjoyed for the ease and ingenuity of Donne's art (see Interpretations, pp. 173-4).

4 **phantasy**   fancy or make-believe rather than reality discovered through reason.

7 **true**   this may mean faithful and might also, in anticipation of 20, convey the idea that she is wonderfully *true* to herself.

9–10 Donne is interested in the movement from soul to body. Here, as in *The Ecstasy* (69), there is the issue of how fitting such a movement is. If the progression from *dreams* to *truths* and *fables* to *histories* (8) is a reasonable one, then might that from dreaming to acting also be natural?

16 **beyond an angel's art**   God, unlike angels, can read the thoughts of the heart. Readers might admire such a daring piece of wit, be surprised at the strangeness of the thought, recoil from its tastelessness, or be interested that he wants to use such language of his beloved.

19–20 See Interpretations, p. 149.

22 **doubt**   fear.

26 **fear, shame, honour**   you might want to ask whether, from a woman's viewpoint, *fear* is justified, and *shame* inevitable once *honour* is lost.

27 **torches**   this is one of those moments when the reader might wonder how far to take this image. Is it a matter of *torches* neatly balancing the earlier image of a *taper* (11)? And can readers exclude the phallic associations of torches and candles?

30 **die**   what areas of meaning are involved here? Is it the traditional association of sleep and death, or, even, the religious associations discussed in the introduction to the poem? For the sexual meaning see *The Canonization*, (21).

The Ecstasy

The Ecstasy resembles both some of the love and the religious poems, except that it seems to lack the edgy ambivalence of the former and the agonizing so often present in the latter.

The poem is metaphysical in both literary and philosophical senses. Conceits are drawn from several branches of learning (literary sense), and it engages with such problems as the union of souls and the relationship between soul and body (the philosophical sense). (See Interpretations, p. 140.) In dealing with the union of souls, Donne imaginatively fashions *soul's language* (22). Do we hear his pleasure in the witty idea of *this dialogue of one* (74)? And perhaps, also, readers, like the one who stands *Within convenient distance* (24), might hear *soul's language* (22) in the music of the verse. The gentle rhythms of reasonable argument, the conclusive cadences at the close of the stanzas and delicate textures such as *But that it first imprints the air* (58) might convince us that this is the refined and elevated language that souls might use (see Interpretations, p. 139).

Title An ecstasy is the temporary departure of the soul from the body. The term, therefore, is not necessarily to be associated with intense sensuous feelings.

In lines 1–28 the lovers sit on a bank, while their souls depart (for the pastoral setting see Context, p. 15). A lover is imagined as standing by. Lines 29–48 deal with what the lover would hear the two souls say about the ecstatic state. Lines 49–76 debate the return of the souls to their bodies.

1–4 This stanza raises a number of issues. Do *pillow* and *pregnant* strongly suggest a sexual reading? The violet's *reclining head* might suggest a posture of sexual compliance, though in Donne's day the violet was an image of modesty and faithfulness. By contrast, the lovers modestly sit. Might *pregnant* merely refer to the shape of the bank?

4 **one another's best** each is equally a wooer and a beloved.

5–6 **cemented/With a fast balm** there are several possible meanings here: their hands are joined by their mutual sweat.

Balm (sweat), according to a contemporary medical idea, keeps bodies from decay (see Context, p. 5). Sweaty palms are a sign of sensuality.

7 **Our eye-beams twisted**   sight, it was believed, either came about because the eye transmitted a beam of light on to an object or received one emitted by an object. Their *eye-beams* twist because *thread* (7) and *string* (8) are made up of twisted fibres to give them strength.

10 **all our means**   what *means* would make them one? The words might either anticipate the union of souls or the union of bodies, discussed in 49–72.

11 **get**   beget. The word might look back to *pregnant* (2) and forward to *propagation* (12) and 37–40 about the transplanted violet. Is such language metaphoric or literal?

13 **Fate**   painters often represented *Fate* as poised above two opposing armies. As with every conceit, it is important to ask which implications of *Fate* and *two equal armies* are appropriate and whether other, perhaps less helpful, ones should be suppressed.

18 **We**   here the lovers are identified more fully with their bodies than their souls. Is this different from the use of *we* in line 51?
   sepulchral statues   statues on a funeral monument.

21–2 See Interpretations, p. 139.

21 **refined**   made pure. The idea, derived from Alchemy, is also present in *concoction* (27).

25 **He**   why did Donne introduce someone who listens? Does he make the reader, who also listens, feel a member of a small and highly privileged group? Is there, perhaps, a hint of the love of display that is present in so many Donne poems?

31 **this**   ecstasy.

32 **what did move**   what motivated or moved us to act.

34 **Mixture**   it was believed that because the soul had so many functions, it was made up of a number of elements. See Context p. 6.

42 **Interinanimates**   a mutual infusion of life with a pun on *anima* (Latin for soul).

44 **loneliness**   the state of being single.
   controls   as in *The Good Morrow* Donne rhymes 'controls' with 'souls'. The rhyme could be no more than a useful

coincidence of sounds or it could reveal Donne's interest in the
relationship between love and power.

45 **know**   might this word show that love is more a matter of
knowledge than emotion? Think about whether love in *A
Valediction: forbidding Mourning* is a matter of reason rather
than passion.

47 **atomies**   atoms.

48 **no change can invade**   as the soul is eternal it cannot change.
The military implications of *invade* raise the issue of whether
metaphors and conceits should be restricted to their immediate
setting or related to language elsewhere in the poem (see lines
13–17 and Interpretations, p. 140).

49 What kind of performance best suits this line: one that
introduces a conscious element of theatricality or one that
reads it as an expression of regret?

50 **forbear**   avoid.

52 **intelligences... sphere**   Aristotle taught that each heavenly
body consists of a sphere governed and moved by a spirit or
intelligence, which inhabits it (see Context, p. 7).

55 **forces, sense**   power of bodily movement, the five senses.

56 **dross... allay**   dross is the waste product of an alchemical
experiment: **allay** is an alloy which is a metal made by
combining two or more metallic elements to give strength.

57–8 Donne might be referring to the idea that stars exert their
influences by working through the air and/or the notion,
present in *Air and Angels*, that angels can only influence people
by appearing in bodies made out of the air.

61–2 See Interpretations, p. 164.

62 **Spirits**   this term was introduced to explain how the body
related to the soul.

64 **subtle knot**   the connection (*knot*) between body and soul is
subtle in the sense that it is so elusive that it resists description
and understanding.

65 **descend**   Once more, there is the issue of how far to press
Donne's language. Do *descend* and *reach* (67) suggest a model of
mutual attraction and co-operation or, given that this is also the
language of the Incarnation, are we also to suppose that the
relationship between body and soul and even the coupling of
lovers can be compared to the birth of the Son of God?

68 Should the *prince* be interpreted as an imprisoned man or, as some have suggested, an unborn child in the womb?

69 It has been suggested that *The Ecstasy* is a poem of seduction. In favour is the fact that the needs of the body have been sounded since line 49, and at this point the poet makes a specific proposal. Against it is the point that nothing in the poem suggests that, in the sexual sense, they are not lovers already. Further, the return of the souls to the bodies does not necessarily mean they are going to make love. The meaning of the poem's last line has an important bearing on this question (see Interpretations, pp. 140-1).

70 **Weak men**   inferior lovers.

71–2 See Interpretations, p. 140.

74 See Context, p. 4.

The Expiration

This was, in 1609, the first of Donne's poems to be printed. An appreciation of this beautiful poem depends upon the reader attending to its aching rhythms and the repetition of its soulful rhymes, which voice the traditional sound of lament – *So* (1), *owe* (5) and *Go* (6).

Title   Three ideas are combined: the loss of breath in kissing, the breathing away of life at the moment of death and a substance being vaporized.

2 See Context, p. 15 and Interpretations, pp. 157-8.

4 **happiest day**   does this simply mean the happiest time of their life, or do the words point to how fleeting their time of love was?

11–12 Does *Except* introduce a clever afterthought which diverts the poet both from the sadness of the situation and his beloved, or does the emphatic alliteration of *double dead* convey an emotional flatness which shows the poet is devastated by the parting?

A Fever

In the opening and close the language of this poem is intimate and tender, whereas in the middle stanzas the writing is philosophically exact (read aloud the fourth stanza), and the beloved is spoken about rather than spoken to (see Interpretations, p. 169). What is to be made of this apparent disparity between feeling and thought? Perhaps the feeling is controlled by the subject matter – anguish at illness and philosophical notions about the end of the world. Perhaps, also, there is thought in the feeling and vice versa. And maybe the poet deliberately turns to argument as a diversion from the pain of the sick-bed. A complicating factor is the stanza form and the rhythms they create, which are ideally suited to the incisive expression of arguments. John Carey calls the rhythms *impudent*. They give the thought a tightly-packaged feel, which may be at odds not only with the emotion of the situation but also with the weighty topics such as death, the end of the world and the nature of the heavens (see Interpretations, p. 167).

1 **die... I** does the internal rhyme enforce the pleading sigh of concern with which the poem opens or does it, by shifting attention to the poet, give the impression that his distress is greater than hers?

6–8 **this world** in line 7 *this world* means the whole universe, whereas in line 8 it means her body. The linking of the microcosmic – the small world of her body – with the macrocosmic – the large world of the universe – is characteristic of metaphysical writing, though such intellectual ingenuity might be emotionally incompatible with the situation of a feverish girl and an anxious lover. See Context, p. 5 and Interpretations, p. 143.

8 **vapours** evaporates. Donne appears to be fascinated by evaporation. (See *The Expiration* (2), *Song: Sweetest love* (25–6) and *A Valediction: forbidding Mourning* (4).) This might be connected with his interest in time and death and / or with his preoccupation with what is material and immaterial, as in his treatment of body and soul.

12 **worms... worthiest**   does the alliteration diminish the world without the beloved (men just become worthy *worms*) and so stress her importance, or is it a deviation from his concern for her into clever games with words?

13–16 See Interpretations, p. 157.

13 **wrangling schools**   in the middle ages groups (called schools) of philosophers debated exactly what kind of fire would burn at the end of the world.

14 **wit**   See Interpretations, pp. 162-3.

19 **corruption**   contemporary medicine taught that fevers only last so long as there is corrupt or decaying matter in the body. The beloved is therefore an ideal figure, a virtuous beauty (see Context, p. 4).

21–4 **meteors... firmament**   *meteors* soon burn themselves out because they are part of the changing world below the moon (see *A Valediction: forbidding Mourning*, line 13), whereas the *firmament* above is permanent, uncorrupted and therefore unchangeable.

25 **seizing**   physical holding and making a legal claim.

The Flea

The vivid presence of the poet, the way the reader is never allowed to forget the flea, and the remarkable way in which the mistress is present throughout, makes this one of Donne's most dramatically visual poems. But immediacy is only one of its pleasures; unlike some of Donne's poems, the argument does not meander but moves carefully, though easily, to its outrageous conclusion. As is often the case in Donne, the argument might be read as an actual attempt to persuade an unwilling woman to comply with the poet's desires, or as an intricate and enjoyable game, played with the woman or the reader or both. The way the crucial words *honour* (26) and *yield'st* (26) are significantly held back to the end of the poem might support the former view, though the skilful contrasts – innocence / guilt, death / life – strengthen the second interpretation. Those who interpret the poem as an attempt at seduction should consider the tone: is it pleading, cajoling, scheming, whining or patronizing? If the poem is a game to be enjoyed for itself, the poet / lover might be adopting the role of the mock preacher (*Mark but this flea* has the ring of a sermon about it) or the pseudo-scholar, who patiently explains a complex matter.

Title   Poems about a lover envying the liberties a flea takes with his
       beloved's body were popular in sixteenth-century European
       poetry. Donne departs from convention by making the flea
       bite the lover as well as the woman and by presenting the
       lover as far more restrained than the flea, who *enjoys before it*
       woo(s) (7).

2   **that**   is his reluctance to name what he desires part of a plan
    to make loss of virginity seem negligible, or is his evasiveness
    intended to stimulate her desire to yield on the grounds that
    that which is not named but strongly implied becomes alluring?

3   **Me... sucked... sucks... thee**   does the *Me / thee* rhyme
    enforce the mutual character of the poem, or does the fact that
    me precedes *thee* point to a basic egocentricity? In *sucked*,
    Donne may have used the old fashioned form of 's', which
    resembles 'f'. If such a play (called an orthographic pun) is
    intended, should it be read as comically indecent, or does it tie
    in with the lover's strategy by feeding her, in a veiled form, the
    word which expresses his intention?

4   **mingled**   a contemporary belief was that blood was *mingled* in
    sexual intercourse.

5   **Confess**   the position and demanding tone of this word raises
    the question (a recurring one in Donne) of whether the poet
    wants to win the girl or the argument. The forceful
    monosyllables of the conclusion – *when thou yield'st to me* (26) –
    might suggest the former, but perhaps *this cannot be said* (5) and
    Yet thou triumph'st, and say'st (23) makes us think about how
    arguments are put into words.

8   **swells**   how far should the connotations of this word be
    pressed beyond its primary meaning of the flea's body swelling
    with their blood? The suggestion of pregnancy (see the first
    stanza of *The Ecstasy*) would surely ruin the lover's strategy.

9 **alas** is this real feeling or a strategy of persuasion? A similar question can be asked of *'Tis true* (25).

10–11 A conceit upon the Holy Trinity. See, also, the note on line 18 and Interpretations, pp. 159-60.

15 **cloistered** is the poet simply being comic by associating sexual union with the chaste life of the cloister, or should the associations of seclusion and special religious status be taken to indicate, as in *A Valediction: forbidding Mourning*, the self-sufficiency of the world of love and the priesthood of lovers?
living walls of jet this is a rare example of Donne writing about nature (compare *Love's Growth*). *Jet* is a black semi-precious stone (see *A Jet Ring Sent*).

16 **use** her habit of denying him.

18 **sacrilege** there may be a witty parallel between the flea, the man and the woman, and the Holy Trinity of Father, Son and Holy Ghost.

19 **Cruel and sudden** the interpretation of the poem will be evident in how these words are performed. The extent to which the anger is assumed will have a bearing upon whether the poem is a game or a serious exercise in wooing.

The Funeral

We must assume that the mistress has given the poet a lock of her hair but has refused to give herself sexually. Does the poet therefore sadly reflect on his lack of success or is he reproachful or even spiteful? Another possibility is that he is fascinated by the business of burial just as much as he is pained by his failure in love. An interesting feature is the language level; on the one hand the poet enjoys the exaggerated language of martyrdom (dying for one's faith) and idolatry (worshipping idols), and on the other there are very casual phrases such as *Whate'er she meant by it* (17).

Title The poem is about a funeral or, more specifically, the preparation of the body for burial. In Donne's day most bodies were buried in shrouds – tough canvas material wrapped round the body and tied at the head and feet. There are some similarities between this poem and *The Relic*, though the occasion of the latter is not burial but the opening up of a grave.

1 **harm** one of the things this poem does is mysteriously suggest that the hair is somehow alive. You might like to relate this to the discussion of the *sinewy thread* of his *brain* (9) and the tension, even paradox, of dead and living things.

2 **Nor question much** is the effect that we do question?

3 **hair** the mention of the lock of hair invites a comparison between this poem and *The Relic*.

6 **Viceroy** one who acts in the place of an absent monarch. See *Holy Sonnet 14* (7).
 which then to heaven being gone is the poet concerned primarily with the grave, the hair and the woman, or does he speak lightly because he knows his soul will be safe in heaven?

7 **control** a favourite word of Donne's, see *The Ecstasy* (44).

8 **her provinces** does the admission that his body is subject to the rule of his mistress (a monarch might talk of ruling his or her provinces) flow naturally from the elevated and detailed way he has spoken of the lock of hair? You might feel it rudely interrupts the line of thought with the uncomfortable reminder that in spite of his persuasive power, the mistress is superior to him.
 dissolution consider the way the poem plays on the idea of corruption. He wishes to corrupt her by seduction, yet her hair preserves his body from the corruption of the grave (*dissolution*).

9–11 These lines depend upon a contemporary idea that the body was held together by sinews which ran from the brain.

14 **except** unless.

19–20 For a discussion of martyrs and relics, see the notes on the titles of *The Canonization* and *The Relic*.

21–4 The reversal at the close is reminiscent of *Woman's Constancy*. Should the reversal be a complete surprise, or should some of the earlier lines be read in a tone of bitter irony so as to anticipate the poem's ending?

21 **humility** subservience.

23 **bravery**   a defiant and rebellious gesture.
24 **bury**   the word may have sexual connotations.

The Good Morrow

This poem (an aubade or a poem set in the morning) makes the event of joyfully waking up with a loved one into an image of awakening into a new, adult life of love. This poem also uses the Renaissance imagery of voyages of exploration and map making (see Context, pp. 2-3). Does this imagery enforce the awakening to a new world of love or do the sea journeys serve as a contrast to the lovers' inner (and more authentic) renaissance? See Context, pp. 1-2.

  2 **we**   compare the transformation of *thou* and *I* into *we* with the way in which *me* and *thee* becomes *our* in *The Flea*. Are there significant differences in tone between these grammatical changes? See Interpretations, pp. 155-6 and p. 172.

  3 **sucked on country pleasures, childishly**   affluent citizens sent their children into the country to be breast-fed by wet nurses. The possible sexual connotations, such as the pun on *country*, might indicate that in their 'childish' state their love was merely physical. See the note on *The Flea* (3) and Interpretations, p. 161.

  4 **seven sleepers**   a legend records that seven Christian youths, who were sealed alive in a cave during persecution by the Emperor Decius, slept for 187 years till they were awakened.

  5 **but this**   compared to this.

10 **controls**   does this word betray a desire in the speaker (in Donne?) to dominate, or could it be a simple acknowledgement that love is so powerful that it can control love of lesser things? Donne displays a characteristic verbal dexterity in the witty idea of love controlling love.

13–14 The sense of the argument is: what does it matter even though... .

15 **appears**   the placing of this word at the end of the line acts out the joyful recognition that each person's face is seen reflected in the other. Should we ignore the suggestion of falseness, of

appearance rather than reality? See Interpretations, p. 145.

18 **sharp north... declining west**   north is a traditional symbol of
coldness and *west* of things in decline. Can the sexual
connotations that she will not be cold and his powers will not
decline be excluded?

19 According to medieval and Renaissance medicine, death occurs
when the elements that make up living things are unequally
mixed (see Context, p. 4).

21 **slacken... die**   should the possible sexual undertones of
slacken (lose vigour) and *die* (loss of sexual power after sexual
consummation) be acknowledged? If they are, do they diminish
the poem by suggesting that love is merely sexual activity or
enrich it through the recognition that sexuality has an
important role? A similar issue is encountered in *The
Canonization*.

A Jet Ring Sent

This poem is untypical of Donne in that it accepts the
conventional attitude of a lover complaining about the cruelty
of his mistress (see Context, p. 15). Nor is there much sense of
intellectual adventure; the poet does not use himself, his
mistress nor the ring as starting-points for ingenious
speculations. Do you find it narrow and disappointing or do you
enjoy its direct, no-nonsense tone, as heard in *Marriage rings are
not of this stuff* (5)?

Title Jet rings were fashionable and quite cheap. They were often
lined with silver and because they could be inscribed they
became popular as love tokens. There is some contemporary
evidence that they were worn on the thumb.

1 **Thou**   the poet frequently addresses the ring as *thou* or *thee*. Is
it more consistently present to him than is the beloved in some
of the other poems? Could it be that the poet addresses his
mistress through the ring because that way he finds it easier to
maintain a steady emotional engagement?
black   a symbol of constancy, because there are no tonal
variations in black.

2 **brittle** inconstant, frail and unserious.

3 **spoke** symbolized. See *Figure* (7).

5 **Marriage rings** these are usually made of gold and so, unlike jet rings, are *precious* (6) and *tough* (6).

7–8 Is the poet artistically pleased with the way the ring so perfectly represents (*Figure*) both their loves, or does he regretfully imply that he wishes it were not such an intellectually and emotionally appropriate image?

8 **Except** unless.

8–9 **fling me away... Yet stay** as well as the contrast between *fling* and *stay* there is probably a pun on *jet* which, by derivation from the French *jette* (to throw), was a medieval word meaning to throw or cast away. See Interpretations, p. 161.
Do you think the contrast is too neat and calculated or does it reveal tenderness in the poet, who, because he has been hurt, is sensitive to others – even rings?

12 **oh** this could be a conventional poetic way of indicating feeling or it could mark a change from subdued or muted grief to uncontrolled anguish.

Lovers' Infiniteness

The emotional tone of this poem is, at times, that of a puzzled and perhaps even vulnerable man, who is anxious about whether his mistress entirely loves him. The poem's argument, however, has a strict mathematical and legalistic character. Is there a tension between feeling and thought? Another feature is that the poem is smoother than those in which harsh rhythms express a forthright speaking voice. See Interpretations, p. 167.

Title Is the infinity that of love itself or the lovers? There is a 1612 setting of a version of this poem by the composer John Dowland.

1 When reading this line aloud you will have to do justice both to the reasoned character of *If* and the (sad? puzzled? despairing?) emotional lilt of the words.

all the poem's central word: 2, 5, 11, 12, 13 (twice), 22, 23, 24, 33. But is it always used with the same shade of meaning and the same emotional weight?

3–4 In love poetry, particularly of the Petrarchan kind (see Context, pp. 15-16), lovers sigh and weep. It is important to ask whether Donne accepts the convention or whether there is a degree of ironic undermining.

5 **treasure... purchase** the idea of wealth which can be measured out becomes one of the controlling images of the poem. Does he intend the poem to work by playing off the image of love as measurable against the common belief that it cannot be measured? You might also ask whether the idea of measuring love is present in the use of *all*?

8 **bargain** although this word might seem gross and cold-blooded, it was used by Elizabethan love poets. For instance, Sir Philip Sidney's *My true love hath my heart and I have his* has this line: *There never was a better bargain driven.*

9 **gift** this word and *gavest* (12) apparently contradict words such as *treasure* (5), *purchase* (5) and *spent* (6). Is this a way of establishing a tension between two ideas of love, or could it be that men pay whereas women give?

16 **stocks** is this meant to contrast unfavourably with the word that applies to his capacity for love – *treasure* (5)?

18 **fears** anxieties and doubts. It is worth asking of this and other poems, how safe the lovers in Donne's poem feel (see Interpretations, p. 150).

21 **ground** in law the crops that grow from a patch of purchased land belong to the new owner.

23 Having said he wanted all her love, he now says he does not want it yet. This is a good place to think about the role of anticipation in both Donne's love and religious poetry. How often do the poems look forward to something rather than celebrate its occurrence in the past or present?

32 **changing hearts** if this is an echo of the Sir Philip Sidney poem quoted above (8), then the poet may be proposing marriage. This would be consistent with *so we shall/Be one*. But as *liberal* could mean speaking openly about sexual matters, he might only be suggesting sexual intercourse.

Love's Alchemy

An angry poem, but at whom or what is the anger directed? The insulting coarseness of *centric happiness* (2) and the dismissive closing couplet might suggest it is a woman or women in general. But it might be love itself, because it has not brought him the joys commonly associated with it (see lines 11–12 on the brevity of sexual pleasure). A third possibility is that it is the elevated language used by poets and lovers. The poem opens with a challenge to speech; those who claim to experience the depths of love should *Say* where it lies. And what is the actual tone of the anger: is it cynical, bitter, disappointed, resentful, envious or even enjoyably self-dramatizing? In thinking over this issue, you need to take account of the poem's abrupt rhythms and abrasive sound textures (see Interpretations, p. 143 and p. 173).

Title Alchemy was a highly complex study, one of the aims of which was to discover, by quasi-chemical means, the philosopher's stone, which would change ordinary metals into gold. As this stone was thought to bestow the power of preservation upon those who possessed it, the title is appropriate: the poet regrets that sexual pleasure is so brief and looks to Alchemy to prolong it (see Context, p. 9).

1–2 *deeper digged love's mine* and *centric happiness* may be crude sexual joking. As a variation of this interpretation, it could be that the poet is using economic exploitation as an analogy of men's sexual enterprises (see Interpretations, p. 171).

3–4 The verbs could express the pride of the sexual athlete and so make the reader recognize him as a man of experience, or they could reduce him to a list of bodily movements carried out in rapid succession in an impersonal and mechanical way.

6 **imposture** a bogus claim.

7 **chemic** alchemist.

8 **pregnant pot** alchemical cauldron in which experiments are prepared.

10 **odoriferous thing, or medicinal** marginally useful by-products of alchemical experiments.

Notes

13 **our**   the change from singular to plural could indicate that the poet is consoling himself by recognizing that he is one of a band of many lovers, or that he has in mind the smaller group, who see through the silly claims of idealistic lovers.

18 **loving wretch**   is the loving wretch a lover or a love poet? Given that the poem is a palinode (a poem that contradicts something written in an earlier poem), could it be that Donne is criticizing something that he himself has said in an earlier poem? If so, which poem, or poems, might he have in mind?

22 **spheres**   the music made by the revolution of the heavens (see Context, p. 7).

23–24   the poet could be saying that, even at their most attractive, women are possessed by demons, or that even the most engaging women are of no more interest or value than dead flesh (*mummy*) once they have been sexually *possessed*.

Love's Growth

As is common in Donne, the astonishing experience of love leads to a philosophical meditation, which is expressed in conceits, drawn from Alchemy, Astronomy and Medicine. Another philosophical element is the traditional conflict between fixed, changeless ideas of perfection and the fact of growth and change. The different modes of speech – intellectual exactitude (7–14), nonchalant observation (11–12) and intimate address, as in line 24, are testing for a performer. Also testing is whether the poem should be delivered as an address to a beloved, a speech to love itself, or a musing soliloquy from which the poet momentarily awakens in 24? For the cadences, see Interpretations, p. 158.

1 **pure**   in Alchemy a substance was *pure* when it was simple and unchangeable.

3 **endure**   undergo.

4 **Vicissitude**   change, alteration.

   grass   grass is a traditional symbol of the decay to which all natural things are subject – *The days of man are as grass, as a flower of the field, so he flourisheth. For the wind goeth over it, and it is gone* (Psalm 103:15–16). Is decay as opposed to growth present anywhere else in the poem, and is its presence or its absence significant?

In 4 the poet has made the discovery (a disturbing or joyful one?) that love is not unchanging but, in the words of the poem, *elemented* (13); that is, part of the changing world of Nature. Compare the idea of love growing with the claim that it is unchanging in *The Anniversary* and *The Good Morrow*.

6   **more**   an important word in the poem (8, 15). See Interpretations, p. 142.

8   **quintessence**   contemporary belief held that all things were made of the four elements: earth, air, fire and water. Some thinkers speculated that there was a fifth element, *quintessence*, which cured all ills, hence line 7.

9   **paining**   this could mean causing pain or having an influence upon soul, or sense.

10   **working**   it was believed that the sun produced warmth, growth and (by implication) a renewal of sexual energy. See also (25).

11–12   These lines are clearly directed at poets (the *Muse* is the source of poetic inspiration). Is there an uneasy relationship between this and other poems by Donne? *The Undertaking*, for instance, sees love as pure and abstract (see Interpretations, p. 168).

14   **do**   might the strong implication of sexual activity exclude other meanings of the word *love*?

19–20   Does the rare use of natural imagery make vivid the beauty of a changing love, or is the reader inevitably reminded, as in *grass* (4), of how short life and love can be?

20   **awakened root**   the phallic implications raise the same question as *do* (14).

23   **spheres**   the heavens were thought of as a set of spheres, all of which had their centre in the earth – hence *concentric* (24), see Context, p. 7.

A painting of Lucy, Countess of Bedford by Isaac Oliver. She lived in Twickenham Park. *Twicknam Garden*, and *A Nocturnal upon S. Lucy's Day* may be connected with her.

A Nocturnal upon S. Lucy's Day, being the shortest day

The reader who wants to appreciate what this poem is saying about loss, grief and feelings of nothingness and negativity should attend to its rhythms and sounds (see Interpretations, p. 143). Crucial to the whole argument of the poem is the phrase *But l am none* (37), which is the start of the last, and possibly most buoyant, stanza, and yet, as a cadence, it is flat and even inert. The co-existence of negatives – *privations* (16), *things which are not* (18) – with the much repeated word *all* raises the question of whether, as a whole, the poem is dark and negative or strangely positive in spite of its subject matter.

Title Until the calendar was altered in 1752, St Lucy's Day
       (13 December) was the shortest of the year. The choice of day

has prompted speculation that Donne wrote the poem for Lucy, Countess of Bedford, either during a severe illness which she suffered in the winter of 1612 / 13 or after her death in 1627 (see illustration on p. 96). The dead beloved might also be Donne's wife, Ann, who died in 1617. There is, however, no reason why an actual event must have prompted the poem.

3 **flasks** the stars were thought to store up light originally given out by the sun and so could metaphorically be spoken of as the *flasks* – powder-flasks – in which gunpowder was kept.

4 **light squibs** the brief flashes and small explosions of a firework.

constant this clearly contrasts with the brief flashes of the *squibs*, but applied to the bereft lover it might mean that without his beloved it is hard to be *constant*.

6 **general balm** either another term for *The world's whole sap* (5) or the preserving substance which, according to some contemporary medical views, prevented decay. *Balm* also soothes and heals (see Context, p. 5).

hydroptic earth the earth, like someone suffering from the disease of dropsy, is full of water and yet insatiably thirsty. It is interesting to speculate why Donne employs this image. See *Elegy 4* (6) and *Holy sonnet 17* and Context, p. 5.

7 **bed's-feet** it was believed that life ebbs away from a dying man towards his feet; it could also mean that a dying man's life – his interests and concerns – shrinks to the dimensions of the bed upon which he lies.

10–18 See Interpretations, pp. 172-3.

10 **Study me then** this raises the familiar problem of sincerity or showiness: is he uncomfortably aware of his extreme condition, or making a self-centred theatrical gesture?

11 What is the effect of the pace of this line and the positioning of *next world* and *spring*? You might read it as a piece of poetic exaggeration or feel that spring, and all it stands for, really is a long way off.

12 See Interpretations, p. 154.

13 **alchemy** alchemy searched for the elixir of life – the essence of life, which cured all ills. Here, however, love produces in him the elixir of death and negativity.

17 The words *ruined* and *re-begot* may allude to the fall of mankind and the salvation, or new birth, brought about by Christ. Are these ideas important in the poem?

21 **limbeck** apparatus used in Alchemy to distil (*draw*) substances.

22–7 These lines are apparently in the fashionable Petrarchan mode; that is, they indulge in dramatic exaggeration such as the tears of lovers drowning the world (see Context, p. 15). There might also be Biblical overtones of Creation and Flood. If so, what is their contribution?

28 The fact that *death* is qualified by the remark that the *word wrongs her* indicates that at this point the poem is concerned with the adequacy of words to their subject matter. Are there are other moments when the subject of the poem becomes the poet's difficulty of expressing exactly what he is feeling? This question can, of course, be asked of other poems.

29 **first nothing** the state of the world before creation may be hinted at here, because Christian doctrine insists that the world was made out of *nothing*.
elixir see note on *alchemy* (13).

31 **prefer** choose.

33 **Some ends, some means** aims or goals (*ends*), and the ways of achieving them (*means*).

34 **some properties invest** all things that exist have distinguishing characteristics.

37 **nor will my sun renew** is he saying that his spiritual winter is so deep that he can expect no spring – no revival of his spirits – or that the sun, the light of life, is identified with his dead beloved?

38 **lesser sun** the real sun.

39 **Goat** the sign of Capricorn which, according to the old Calendar, the sun enters on 12 December. The goat is traditionally associated with *lust* (40).

41 This line is very much a case of how performance affects interpretation. Should it be read self-pityingly, enviously or in a spirit of generous recognition of others' good fortune?

42 **festival** this word introduces a sustained conceit based upon religious ritual – *prepare* (43), *hour* (44), *vigil* (44), *eve* (44). The poet could be commemorating her and thinking upon himself

at the darkest time of the year, or preparing himself to meet her in death.

45 **is**   a paradox of this poem is that though it is built on negatives it ends with *is*.

The Relic

There are two interesting tensions in this poem. The first is the very strong contrast between the poem's opening with its graphic preoccupation with graves and bones and the completely spiritual love celebrated at the close. The second is the familiar one in Donne of elevated claims about love and the poem's light movement, diverting asides and flippant dismissals. *The Relic* resembles *The Canonization* in that the lovers become objects of religious devotion, and the large claims advanced through the central conceits are ingeniously shown to be appropriate to the earthly love the couples enjoy. For tone and viewpoint see Interpretations, p. 142.

Title   Relics are the bones or belongings of saints, the veneration (honouring) of which was an important aspect of medieval Catholicism. The Thirty-nine Articles, which set out doctrine for the Church of England, said that the *Worshipping and Adoration of relics is a fond (foolish) thing, vainly invented, and grounded upon no warranty of Scripture, but rather repugnant to the Word of God*. As with the religious poems, it is interesting to ask whether Donne still thinks as a Catholic or whether he adopts the official Anglican point of view. The word *mis-devotion* (13) suggests the poem is Anglican, but the imagery might show that his imagination is still Catholic (see Interpretations, pp. 152-3).

1–2   It was a common practice to bury bodies in old graves.
broke   this word could serve as a foil to the surprising note of courtesy in the second line, or its harshness might indicate the resentment lovers feel at being disturbed in their happy isolation. See *alone* (7).

3 **woman-head**   the primary meaning is the way women behave, but there might also be a play on maidenhead.

5 **spies**   does the poet resent being spied upon, or is there a barely concealed delight in being seen? This issue is also present in *The Canonization* and *The Sun Rising*.

6 **bracelet of bright hair**   a love token of fair hair. Since her hair is the only part of her in the grave, it is surprising that the poet speaks so confidently about a loving couple (8).

10–11 **the last busy day**   the Day of Judgement when, in Christian belief, at the second coming of Christ, bodies arise from their graves to be re-joined with their souls (see *Holy sonnet 7*). Does the language used here devalue the idea of the Last Judgement by reducing it to a busy day, or does it reveal a touching desire on the part of the poet that, even at the climax of world history, there should be time for lovers to meet?

12 **fall**   occur.

16 **to make**   In the light of the prosaic *he that digs us up* (14), the transformation of the lovers into saints might appear ludicrous, but, given that it is Donne's idea that the *Bishop and the King* pronounce them saints, could it be that he enjoys, and thereby endorses, this promotion to sainthood?

17 **Mary Magdalen**   St Mary Magdalen was a follower of Jesus who, in the imagination of the Church, has become identified with the prostitute, who, in St Luke's Gospel, washes Jesus's feet and dries them with her hair. She is usually portrayed as having long, flowing hair.

18 Might the poet be identified with Christ? There was certainly one tradition that Christ and Mary Magdalen were in love. Christopher Ricks observed that Jesus Christ has the same syllabic count as *something else*. But there are alternatives. He could be regarded as another saint or, jokingly, as one of Mary Magdalen's lovers – a very unlikely candidate for sainthood. Above all, the difficulty is that in the New Testament Christ's tomb is empty, so there would be no bones in it. It may be that the problem should be looked at from another angle: could it be that the poet jokingly mocks the age of *mis-devotion* for mistaking him for Christ and for thinking that his chaste beloved might be a prostitute?

19 **and some men**   the joke is that women are supposed to be more superstitious than men.

21 **paper**   poem.

22 **miracles**   relics of saints were believed to bring about miracles.

25–6 The belief referred to here is that each person is watched over by his or her own guardian angel. Angels were commonly believed to have no sexual characteristics.

27–8 A kiss of greeting and a kiss when parting was a common practice that implied no sexual interest between people.   For the importance of the chaste kiss, see Context, p. 13.

29–30 Where does the poem stand over the matter of chastity? The miracle could be that the two overcame the temptation to touch *the seals* (sexual organs). Another possibility is that *injured* might imply that *late law* has done nature wrong, and that, therefore, the poet is regretting intercourse is prohibited.

31–3 See Interpretations, p. 162.

32 **pass**   surpass.

Song: Go, and catch a falling star

It is hard to disagree with Coleridge's judgement (found in his notebooks) of this vigorous and forthright poem: 'Life from crown to sole'. The poet takes pleasure in his own gusto. In the poem's restless rhythms and its pose of disengaged cynicism, we might hear the poet enjoying the absurdity that a woman could be both beautiful and faithful (see Interpretations, p. 150). But perhaps the possibility of there being such a woman gives the poem life.

1–9 Listing impossible activities was a feature of contemporary love poetry (see Context, p. 15). Donne might be mocking the absurdity of this convention by asserting that *a woman true, and fair* (18) does not exist. Though it might be that he playfully relishes the prospect of such fantastic exploits.

1 **Go**   is this addressed to a would-be lover who believes in female fidelity, a fellow poet or an adventurer who seeks wonders?

falling star   since falling star(s) – shooting stars – were thought to be signs of impending disaster, it could be that the impossibility the poet has in mind is controlling fate.

2 **mandrake root**   the idea of making a mandrake root, which resembled the human shape, pregnant is absurd in at least two ways: legend has it that when pulled up its scream kills those who hear it, and, in some cases, it resembles the male and not the female form.

4 **the Devil's foot**   the devil is commonly represented as having a cloven hoof. To ask who *cleft* it is to engage in an occult version of the highly speculative questions that fascinated medieval theologians, and, in some poems, Donne.

5 **mermaids**   mermaids, or sirens, were thought to lure sailors on to rocks by their beautiful singing. The line may reveal heroic ambitions: does he want to be like the Greek hero, Odysseus, who, because be was tied to a mast, heard the sirens yet survived?

8 **wind**   a favourable wind for sailors.

9 **honest**   this could refer specifically to a true and faithful lover or, more generally, to the honest person who has no hope of advancement in a corrupt world.

10 **be'est born to**   have an inclination to.
strange sights   neither here nor in *strange wonders* (15) is there an attempt to convey the feel of strangeness or wonder. Perhaps wonder is impossible because there are no *strange sights*. Perhaps the poet is concealing his disappointment.

11 **Things invisible to see**   the reading of this crucial line affects the interpretation of the poem. Does the poet play with an oxymoron (a verbal contradiction) or is he drawn to the paradox of being able to see that which is invisible? Compare *The Undertaking* 17–20.

18 **true, and fair**   is the poem weakened because it unquestioningly accepts this (typically male) idea? Perhaps, however, in the cadence of *true, and fair* there is the momentary and joyful glimpse that such a person may exist.

20 **pilgrimage... sweet**   in contemporary literature lovers were often spoken of as pilgrims. Again, does this word, albeit momentarily, suggest the possibility that there actually is a woman *true, and fair*? If so *sweet* should be read without irony.

22 **next door** consider the effect of this familiar, domestic term
in a poem about heroic tasks and *All strange wonders* (15). Is it
cynicism – he will not even go next door to see a woman who
might be *true, and fair* – or cheerful resignation to a world
without such *wonders*?

27 **ere I come** what does he want of the woman who might be
true, and fair? Would he admire or court her?
two, or three does this reveal regret or dismissive cynicism?

Song: Sweetest love, I do not go

This poem is uncharacteristic of Donne in that there is little
philosophizing, and the rhythms of the verse, unlike, for
instance, *Song: Go, and catch a falling star*, are smooth and
mellifluous (see Interpretations, p. 157). What it does share with
other poems is a preoccupation with parting, an anxiety about
time and the problem of whether the poet consistently tries to
comfort his beloved or becomes distracted by his own ideas (see
Interpretations, p. 142). For a discussion on the poem's treatment
of death, see Interpretations, p. 146.

Title In his *Life of Donne*, Isaac Walton claims that this poem, along
with *A Valediction: forbidding Mourning*, was written in 1611
shortly before Donne parted from his wife to travel on the
Continent.

1–8 See Interpretations, p. 168.

4 **fitter** is this a compliment or, given *me* at the end of the line,
concealed egotism?

8 **feigned deaths** is this moving because it is an ineffectual joke
offered in the hope of cheering up his beloved, or is there the
uncomfortable implication that if his deaths are *feigned*, his
grief at parting may also be fake?

11 The sun has neither will (*desire*) nor awareness (*sense*).

13–14 **fear not me/But believe** perhaps an echo of *Fear not, believe
only*, St Luke 8:50.

16 **wings and spurs** he could be casting himself in the role of

Mercury – the winged messenger of the Greek and Roman gods.

17 **feeble**   this marks a decisive change of tone. It could make the poem seem inconsistent or could be read as a deliberate restraint after the poetic flights of fancy in the second stanza.

19 **Cannot add**   perhaps an echo of St Matthew 6: 27: *Which of you by taking care, is able to add one cubit unto his stature?* Coleridge praised this poem for its religious thoughtfulness and faith, possibly because of its awareness, both here and in 17, of human limitation.

21–4 Consider how the structure of the stanza makes these lines different in their effectiveness and significance from the preceding four lines. This question may also be asked of other stanzas in the poem.

23 **teach it art and length**   give it cunning (*art*) and allow it scope (*length*).

25–32 When reading this poem aloud, particular attention must be given to bringing out the significance of the assonance on 'i'. Elsewhere in the poem, the long and short 'e' sounds help to establish the tone.

26 **sigh'st my soul away**   sighing was believed to shorten life.

27 **unkindly kind**   should this phrase (an oxymoron or verbal contradiction) be seen as a clever phrase offered by the poet to cheer up his beloved or does its very ingenuity weaken the point that although her tears are natural (*kind*) they might harm him (*unkindly*)?

32 **the best of me**   my very self.

33 **divining**   foreseeing the future.

34 **Forethink**   Donne quite often forethinks – speaks with assurance about what will happen in the future (see Interpretations, pp. 148-9).

36 **fears**   are they just her fears?

38 **turned aside to sleep**   compare this with the closing three stanzas of *A Valediction: forbidding Mourning*. Do you think a poem about parting is more effective when it uses familiar, domestic details such as the couple turning aside from each other to sleep, or does the strange appropriateness of the compasses conceit get closer to the idea that though apart they are not really parted?

The Sun Rising

This poem opens like *The Canonization* with an outburst against an intruder upon the intimate world of the lovers and it closes (as does *The Relic*) by establishing a link between the world of their love and the world at large. Yet there are features that make this poem quite distinctive. One such feature is the masculine, possessive pride the lover takes in his beloved. Coleridge responded to this aspect when he wrote: 'Fine, vigorous exaltation, both soul and body in full puissance'. In the full joy of possessing his beloved, he extravagantly claims that their love is so intensely real that it constitutes the basic reality of the world, even to the point of saying *Nothing else is* (22). Perhaps the strength of the poem is that he almost compels us to agree with him.

Title Like *The Good Morrow* this is an aubade, a song sung in the morning.
1 Does the poet adopt the role of the young rebel deriding the older and feebler generation, or might he be anticipating stanza three by speaking in an authoritative and even kingly tone?
3 **curtains** probably those round a four-poster bed rather than at the windows.
5–8 Are these lines contemptuously dismissive of people whose activities are banal, or do they show that he finds them interesting, purposeful and attractive?
5 **saucy** impertinent with possibly a hint of lechery.
   pedantic in the manner of a schoolmaster.
7 **court-huntsmen** members of the court who hunt or self-seekers who hunt for a position or promotion at court. Both senses could be combined: James I was fond of early morning hunting, so those wishing to curry favour would be up early to join him (see Context p. 14).
8 **country ants to harvest offices** this probably means hardworking farmers, engaged in harvesting.
9–10 These lines explore the tension between praise of a permanent, unchanging state and a fascination with the variety of the

physical world, which is subject to time and change. Does the elevated tone and the measured, majestic pace convince you that an eternal and unchanging state is both superior and desirable, or does the vividness of *rags of time* direct you to the keen pleasures, albeit fleeting ones, that are to be found in the world? This tension is central to Donne's poetry.

9 **Love, all alike**   love which never changes.

13 **wink**   the basic meaning in the seventeenth century was a closing of the eye, though the meaning of a discreet and knowing signal was also available.

14 **her sight**   sight of her.

15 **eyes**   poets conventionally wrote of the brightness of their beloved's eyes and frequently compared them to the sun.

17 The East Indies produced spices, and the West Indies were mined for gold. The images could suggest her alluring richness, or the poet might regard his beloved as an object to be exploited (see Context, p. 2).

20 **hear... here**   perhaps the playfulness of the echo indicates the intellectual superiority of the poet over the sun?

21 The swelling movement of this line might express the lover's (understandable) possessive pride in such a beautiful woman. Might it also reveal his desire to control and dominate?

22 **Nothing else is**   in the light of the introductory remarks, perhaps we should ponder whether these emphatic words really insist that the love the couple share is the only fundamental reality (see Interpretations, p. 154).

23 **play**   does this word raise the issue of who is doing the playing? A similar question is raised by *mimic* (24).

24 **alchemy**   dazzling but superficial.

25 **half**   since the sun is single he can only be half as happy as the couple.

29 **Shine**   the order to *shine* on the lovers is a dramatic change from the opening, where the sun's intrusion was resented. Is there a progression from anger to acceptance?

30 **centre... sphere**   Donne employs a geocentric rather than a heliocentric picture of the world (see Context, p. 9). We might say that though it is not scientifically correct, it is still our everyday experience that the sun does indeed appear to move around the earth.

The Triple Fool

In some respects this is a light poem: it is humorously directed against the poet himself, several of its lines are short, and some of the rhyming couplets could even be described as snappy. Yet it gives a quite detailed consideration of important matters: how the discipline of art (in this case poetry) controls personal feeling, and how art in performance can awaken in a listener the feelings that inspired the artist. To put it another way: the writer is lover, poet and listener. See Interpretations, p. 175.

Title The occasion is a musical performance of one of the writer's poems. The title invites us to ask in what ways the poet is a triple fool (see Context, p. 14).

4 **wiseman** not only someone who is wise but also the person who appears wise in the ways of the world.

5 **deny** is this weak self-justification or is it a much tougher and more knowing recognition that if he were successful in love, even the *wiseman* would envy him?

6–7 The popular belief was that sea water is salty but land water fresh, because land water had passed through subterranean passages in which it lost its saltiness. The language conveys a very strong sense of the inner life of the poet, suggesting through the image of *earth's inward narrow crooked lanes* the secret depths of the self and the mysterious processes that occur in the mind.

10–11 See Interpretations, pp. 156-7.

10 **numbers** a common term for poetry.

22 You may feel that the ending is good because it takes up the theme of wise men and fools or that its proverb-like quality is out of keeping with the narrative character of the poem.

Twicknam Garden

This zestful poem enjoyably plays with the renaissance conventions of the distraught lover / poet. There is a dramatic mismatch between the seasons and mood of the poet, and his weeping appears to be perpetual. It is difficult to tell whether the pain of an unrequited lover can be felt in and through the self-conscious display of the poetic persona (see Interpretations, pp. 142-3 and p. 175).

Title Twicknam Park was the home from 1607 of Donne's patroness, Lucy, Countess of Bedford. The garden was elaborately laid out on a symmetrical plan, which represented the geocentric image of the universe (see Context, p. x). Lucy's garden did not contain fountains, but Donne might have been familiar with them from other formal gardens.

1–5 The changing rhythms of these lines could mark the depth of his anguish, or indicate an element of self-parody.

2 **spring** in poetry moods are frequently compared and contrasted with the seasons.

4 **balms** medicinal preparations which soothe and heal. Donne also alludes to extreme unction – the annointing of the eyes before death.

6 **spider love** it was believed that a spider changed everything it ate into poison.

transubstantiates the Roman Catholic Church taught that Christ's presence in the Mass was brought about by a change in the substance of the bread, so that although it looked unchanged its real nature had been transformed. This doctrine was called transubstantiation. See Interpretations, p. 151 and p. 163.

7 **manna to gall** the children of Israel were fed in the desert by the miraculous appearance of a bread-like food called *manna*. Hence in Christian symbolism *manna* is a foreshadowing and sign of the holy communion or mass. *Gall* is a sharp-tasting herb which throughout the Bible symbolizes bitter experience.

Converting *manna to gall* is a reversal of the action of the mass and might also be a subversion of the poetic convention that love is a religion.

9 **True paradise... the serpent** according to the book of Genesis in the Bible, Adam and Eve were expelled from the Garden of Eden, or paradise, because they yielded to the serpent's temptation.

10 **wholesomer**   better in the sense of more fitting and more appropriate.

11 **Benight**   overcome with darkness.

15 **nor yet leave loving**   what is to be made of the poet's desire to continue loving and yet avoid its pain (*senseless* means without sensation)? Does it successfully show a man in the paradoxical state of hating the pain of love yet longing to continue loving? Perhaps it shows a liking for strange and extreme states.

17 **mandrake**   a plant which was supposed to scream when uprooted. See *Song: Go, and catch a falling star* (2).

19–25   What is the relationship between the poet's emotions and the imagery? Are his feelings momentarily allayed by the ingenuity of the fountain image before they break out in *Alas, hearts...* , or is that outburst as staged as the image (a comic one?) of lovers tasting their mistress's tears?

19 **vials**   tear-vessels.

20 **love's wine**   possibly a reference to wine consecrated in the mass.

27–8   The close of the poem might be an anguished image of the poet's misfortune in loving a woman who, unlike all others, is faithful to someone else. There might also be a hint of comedy in the absurd situation of loving the one woman who will remain faithful.

The Undertaking

There is a puzzling tension between the elevated subject and the poem's form and tone. The poem celebrates *loveliness within* (13), and yet the metre is brisk, and the tone proud, boasting and perhaps even smugly self-satisfied. A further aspect of this tension is that between the refined character of the love and the terse, philosophical force of the argument. These disparities were noted by Coleridge, who wrote: 'A grand poem; and yet the tone, the riddle character, is painfully below the dignity of the main thought'. See Interpretations, p. 142 and p. 168.

Notes

Title   An alternative title is *Platonic Love*. Platonism taught that what
        is visible is only a dim reflection of the real world, which exists
        in an eternal and unchangeable form (see Context, pp. 12-13).
        For Platonists, it follows that the highest kind of love ignores
        the body and seeks only the mind, because it is more akin to
        the eternal and unchanging world. The contrast between the
        material world and the real world is present in a number of
        Donne's poems.

   1   **braver**   finer, more glorious and more impressive.

   2   **Worthies**   the *Worthies* were nine heroic figures who
        exemplified all the qualities of ideal warriors. In public
        pageants they were represented by men, who loudly boasted
        about the *Worthies'* marvellous deeds.

   4   **hid**   it is unusual to find a poem celebrating secrecy when so
        many of Donne's poems are showy and theatrical. Does the
        poet keep his secret hidden?

 5–8   See Interpretations, p. 160.

   6   **specular stone**   a transparent stone used in building ancient
        temples. Since Donne and his contemporaries believed that it
        was no longer available, there was no point in learning the very
        difficult art of cutting it.

   8   **cut**   a reader must do justice to the particularly incisive stress
        on this word.

  13   See Interpretations, p. 150.

14/16 **loathes / oldest clothes**   do you think the poet finds it easy
        to dismiss colour and skin as *clothes*, which are to be loathed?
        You might also ask whether the insistence of the rhyme
        creates the impression that *inner loveliness* matters more than
        the flesh.

  17   **as I have**   see *Twicknam Garden* (19–22) for another view of
        the poet as a pattern of true love.

  18   **Virtue attired**   if you have decided that *oldest clothes* make the
        flesh faded and uninteresting, is it possible to respond
        positively to the image of *Virtue* clothed in a *woman*?

  19   **say**   does the poet's real achievement lie not in loving but in
        saying? See Interpretations, p. 162.

  20   **the He and She**   as the sentence starts with a questioning *If*
        (17), is there a hint that the poet acknowledges that it is very
        difficult to ignore sexuality?

22 **profane men** poets often spoke of love as a religion and of ordinary lovers as irreligious or *profane*. See also the second stanza of A *Valediction: forbidding Mourning* and Interpretations, p. 149.

A Valediction: forbidding Mourning

The relationship between reason and emotion in this poem is particularly enigmatic: is it an argument touched by emotion, or a lovingly intimate poem that controls feeling by expressing it in the form of an argument?

Title A valediction is a poem of farewell. If Isaac Walton is right in saying that this poem was written by Donne when he parted from his wife for a journey to France in 1611, the *I* of the poem may be the poet himself. If, however, this is a guess, both the *I* and *thou* could be fictional. Would this make a difference?

1–8 See Interpretations, p. 164.
As this word often introduces an argument: might it also introduce a more emotional kind of speech?
virtuous men those with a clear conscience die peacefully.

5 **melt** think about the force of this word in the light of its common meaning in Donne's day of yielding to an emotion or giving way to tears. Consider, also, its importance in the poem in relation to the plea for *firmness* (35).

6 See Context, p. 15.

8 See Interpretations, p. 149.

11 **trepidation** the system of astronomy originated by Ptolemy (see Context, pp. 6-7) held that the spheres surrounding the earth trembled (*trepidation*) as they revolved; this affected the motion of the planets but was neither felt nor caused damage on earth. It was, thus, *innocent* (12); that is to say, harmless.

13 **Dull sublunary lovers** since the Fall ruined the region below the moon, earthly lovers are tarnished (see a fuller explanation of this belief in Context, p. 7).

14 **(Whose soul is sense)** *sublunary lovers* are *dull* because their

affections originate from, and are entirely controlled by, the
senses.

17 **refined** purified (see Interpretations, p. 163).

20 **Care less** what force do these words have, given that the poet
lingers over *eyes, lips, and hands* before coming to the word *miss*?
(See Interpretations, p. 141.)

24 **aery thinness beat** gold beaten to a near transparent state to
produce gold leaf.

25–36 In Donne's day compasses performed the tasks now carried out
by both dividers and compasses. Three uses are present here:
measuring or dividing the distance between two points;
opening and subsequently closing the compasses in the course
of taking a measurement, and drawing a circle. See Context,
p. 3 and Interpretations, p. 164 and p. 173.

   The precision and detail of this conceit provokes a number
of questions. Does the detail enhance or detract from the poem
as a whole? Is the precision an embodiment of the firm control
of emotion for which the poet so beguilingly pleads? Is the
conceit too cold and austere? Is the attention necessary to
appreciate the conceit out of proportion to the space it
occupies in the poem? For a visual representation of compasses
see illustration on p. 3. See Interpretations, p. 164.

36 **end, where I begun** is the image of a circle being completed
less satisfactory as a symbol of homecoming than the closing of
compasses (29–36)?

A Valediction: of Weeping

Parting before a journey is the subject of several Donne poems.
As in the case of *Song: Sweetest love* and *A Valediction: forbidding
Mourning*, this poem makes the standard poetic connections
between sea and tears and wind and sighs. Yet whereas these
connections were passing references in the *Song* and the
mourning *Valediction*, here the conceit of tears is the chief
matter of the poem. And as the chief matter, other conceits
(perhaps all of them) are derived from it. Donne draws our

attention to this by saying of tears that they are *emblems of more*
(7). Understandably, J.B. Leishman called the poem 'fiendishly
ingenious'. Is it any more than that?

Title   Weeping and tears were popular subjects in sixteenth- and
     seventeenth-century poetry. See Context, p. 15 and
     Interpretations, p. 174.

   2   **My tears**   readers need to work out who is weeping and when.

3–4   Look through these lines to see how the image of tears
     produces a conceit on coins.

   6   **pregnant**   what is it about this image that makes it appropriate
     at this point in the poem? The same question can be asked of
     line 2 in *The Ecstasy*.

   7   **emblems of more**   see the introductory note.

   8   **that thou**   that person.

   9   **nothing** consider the emotional impact of this word in the
     poem as a whole. If they are nothing, then there are no tears
     and if no tears, no poem.
     divers shore   in a different country.

10–13   Edward Wright (1558–1615) worked out the mathematics that
     enabled mapmakers to project flat shapes onto a sphere. The
     workman (11) had to use several sheets of paper (*copies*).

  13   **nothing**   Because a *globe* (16) is round it is like a nought and is
     therefore *nothing*.

  16   **impression**   see note on lines 3–4.

17–18   A conceit based on the Biblical Flood (Genesis: 6–9) is present
     here.

  18   **my heaven**   the poet's beloved.

  20   **draw not up seas**   the moon controls the tides.

  21   **in thine arms**   what is the effect of knowing that he is lying in
     her arms?

  26   **one another's breath**   the mutual breathing (and, of course,
     kissing) of couples was used as an image of the departure of
     breath in dying, hence *hastes each other's breath*, (27). See *The
     Expiration*.

Woman's Constancy

This poem is a game played between poet, mistress and reader, with neither mistress nor reader being quite sure what the poet is going to say next. We are not sure, because the poem seems to combine an edgy uncertainty with an impulse to mock and ridicule. Reading the poem aloud might bring out the difficulties of judging its tone. How, for instance, should *whole* (1), *now* (4) and *just* (5) be delivered? For the drama of the poem, see Interpretations, p. 155.

Title How applicable is the title?

2 **when thou leav'st** is the tone one of sad resignation in the face of female infidelity, or can you detect the deliberate adoption of the pose of a hurt man?

   say it is important to ask whether the real subject matter is not what people do but the words they use (see Interpretations, p. 162).

3 **antedate** to assign an earlier date to an event or agreement.

4–13 Do the four sentences beginning with *Or* suggest the lady's remarkable capacity for argument, the poet's bitter realization of just how fickle the lady is, or are they arguments the man puts into the lady's mouth in order to prepare for the reversal with which the poem ends?

10 **sleep, death's image** it was a poetic convention that sleep was akin to death.

14 **lunatic** she might be a lunatic because she foolishly wants to abandon her lover or because, like the moon, she is changeable.

   'scapes tricks or wiles often prompted by sexual motives.

15 **Dispute, and conquer** is the aggressively masculine edge of these words blunted by the nonchalant and even indifferent tone of the couplet in which they appear?

16 **abstain** how surprising is his refusal to tackle the arguments of his fickle mistress? Might we reflect that the poem has shown that the words of lovers are unreliable?

Elegy 4: The Perfume

This poem is akin to a domestic comedy such as was written by Donne's contemporary, Ben Jonson. An adventurous young man courts a girl, who, in the traditions of comedy, is locked up by her jealous family, but although he evades the *hydroptic father* (6), the *immortal mother* (13) and *The grim eight-foot-high iron-bound serving-man* (31) (all of them like characters from a comedy) he is, with delightful comic irony, given away by his own *loud perfume* (41). Donne creates a distinctive persona, whose enterprising but luckless escapades are related in appropriately rough couplets. Perhaps there are moments, so common in Donne, when an interest in arguments and ideas dilutes the psychological consistency of the persona. For the setting of the poem, see Context, p. 14, and for a discussion of the couplet form, see Interpretations, pp. 166-7.

2 **escapes** adventurous escapades of an amorous nature.
3–6 The tone of hurt outrage is evident in the spiteful remark about her *hydroptic* (6) (suffering from dropsy) father, yet perhaps there is also pride and even enjoyment in being singled out as the object of her father's anger? Does the emphatic swagger of *So am I* (5) indicate his pleasure at being the centre of interest? See Context, p. 5.
3 **at bar** in a criminal court the accused stands at the bar.
7 –8 The *cockatrice* or basilisk is a kind of lizard which was believed to kill by its looks. Is her father so fierce that he can even kill a cockatrice, or are his eyes so old and his vision so bleary (*glazed* could have that meaning) that spying on the lovers is as likely to be as successful as trying to outstare a *cockatrice*?
11 **Hope of his goods** Who is after what? The young man might be accusing the father of only being interested in his daughter's price on the marriage market. He might also be quoting the father's view that the lover is only interested in her riches. And what does the reader make of the lover? Is he a trustworthy man motivated by love or a daring opportunist out for sexual pleasure?

14 **buried in her bed** a play on the traditional association between the grave and the bed.

18 **rings... armlets** love tokens.

20 **swoll'n** pregnant. See note on *The Flea* (8).

21–2 The mother is closely watching her daughter for signs of pregnancy such as a pale complexion or a sudden liking for a particular food.

23 **politicly** scheming with the ulterior motive of securing a confession of guilt from her daughter.

25–26 This couplet brings the poem very close to comedy. Many comic plots depend upon the ability of the young to *gull* (deceive, mislead or cheat) unwary adults. Audiences are usually invited to find the adventurous young attractive. Is that the case here?

29 **ingled** dandled or fondled by their father.

34 **Rhodian Colossus** the Colossus of Rhodes (one of the seven wonders of the ancient world) was an enormous statue that was said to stand across the entrance to Rhodes harbour.

41 **loud** look through the poem for words that are a contrast to *loud*.

47–9 The *isle* of Britain, where the native beasts are cattle and dogs rather than the exotic *unicorn*.

52 **oppressed** this probably refers to pressing prisoners with heavy weights to make them talk.

53–70 Perhaps the simulated fury of this long denunciation of perfume contributes to the comedy of the poem. Do we also feel Donne's intellectual pleasure in formulating such a dramatic and intricate expression of the persona's plight?

57 **Base excrement** it was a popular joke that perfume was merely the excretion of flowers and animals.

59 **silly amorous** a foolish lover.

64 **substantial** real, solid things overlooked by those in a Prince's court, who are distracted by empty fashion.

67–8 **simply... joined** things made up of loathsome separate (*simply*) entities are no better when made into a compound (*joined*).

70 **rare** good things are universal not unusual (*rare*) as is perfume.

71–2 Perhaps the closing couplet has the quality of an afterthought.

It does, however, return to the plight of the lover being
frustrated by the father and provides, with a dash of grim wit, a
new use for the perfume.

72 **corse** corpse.

Elegy 5: His Picture

This elegy observes some of the conventions of contemporary
poetry: separated lovers are spoken of as *dead* (3), and those
united by a deep love speak of themselves as superior to *rival
fools* (11). What makes it characteristically Donne's is its blend of
vivid physical detail and quasi-theological argument. As so often
in Donne, the balance or tension of these elements gives the
poem life. See Interpretations, p. 166 and p. 170-1.

1 **picture** miniature portraits, often no wider than 4 to 5
centimetres, were commonly given as parting gifts.

3 **dead** can this be read both metaphorically and literally?

4 **shadows** a picture could be spoken of as a shadow. A ghost
or shade could also be called a shadow.

5–10 Perhaps because writing as visual as this is rare in Donne,
readers might find these lines more interesting, and even more
convincing, than the passage that follows about how love can
look beyond appearances to the inner self.

10 **powder** gunpowder.

13 **This** the portrait.
and thou shalt say how convincing is this? Does he have
complete confidence in the maturity of her love and so can
predict how she will react, or is he aware of how repulsive he
might be and so is leading her to respond in a way which is
favourable to him?

18 **milk** in the Bible and in much religious literature it is
common to draw a distinction between the spiritually young
who, like babies, need milk and the mature who can feed on the
real meat of religion. For instance: *I gave you milk to drink, and
not meat*, I Corinthians 3:1.

Elegy 16: On his Mistress

The beloved's wish to accompany the poet makes her more like the heroine of a romantic, even a Shakespearean, comedy, who disguises herself in order to be with the man she loves. Donne, however, departs from the plot conventions of romantic comedy by having the lover persuade his beloved not to adopt the role of the disguised heroine. It is a highly wrought piece with many repetitions and carefully paced climaxes, yet, as with many Donne poems, such an elaborate patterning in the language exists alongside what seems to be genuine feeling; note, for instance, the touching simplicity of the close.

  1 **fatal**   this word could point to the depth of their love by implying that even at their first meeting (*interview*) they were destined for each other, and it might also anticipate the fears of his death, which are the subject of lines 50–4.
  3 **remorse**   the tenderness and pity she feels for him.
  4 **my words' masculine persuasive force**   so much of Donne is in these words: a self-centred celebration of his prowess in loving, a knowledge of how his beloved will respond to his persuasion, and, given *words'*, an awareness of the power of his poetry. See Interpretations, p. 150 and p. 170.
  7 **calmly**   should the poet be believed when he says he begs *calmly*?
  8 **want and divorcement**   her absence from him due to separation.
 11 **overswear**   swears oaths of constant love again and again.
 14 His insistence that she should not disguise herself and follow him is consistent with his firm statement in line 12 that she *shalt not love by ways so dangerous*. It is difficult to know how a reader should respond. Do we admire his concern that she be treated with the dignity of a *true mistress*, or might we regret that he is denying her the brave and enterprising role of the *feigned page*?
 16 **only**   this means either that she is the only one who could

rouse in him the *thirst* (17) to return or that that is the only role she can play.

19 **move** remove.

21–3 Donne appears to be recasting a Greek myth here: instead of *Boreas* (21) – the north wind – carrying away a girl called *Orithea* (23), he makes *Orithea* a tree or plant, which is *in pieces shivered* (22) by *Boreas*.

24 **proved** undergone or suffered.

25 **unurged** without compulsion or necessity.

27 **Dissemble nothing** the immediate meaning is: do not disguise yourself. Can, however, the idea of other sorts of deception be excluded?

28 **strange** to be either a stranger or to be someone whose identity is concealed. *Strange* has appeared in line 1.

30 This line can be usefully compared with line 4. We might also ask whether such polarized understandings of men and women are found in other poems?

31 **apes** fools. The point of comparison is based on the proverb that apes are still apes even if they are richly dressed.

33 **chameleons** in the same way that chameleons change their colour, so the French change their moods.

34 **Spitals of diseases** a spital is a hospital, which treated venereal diseases.

35 **Love's fuellers** those who stoke up their own passions.

36 **players** the poet criticizes the French for being players, but he and his beloved might also be said to play.

37 **know** does the poet successfully play upon the two meanings of *know* – recognize and have sexual intercourse with?

38 **indifferent** oblivious as to whether his lust is satisfied by either man or woman.

41 **Lot** in Genesis 19: 4–11 the men of Sodom are so aroused by two angels who visit Lot that they demand that Lot hand them over so they can satisfy their lust.

42 **spongy hydroptic** see *A Nocturnal upon S. Lucy's Day, being the shortest day* (6). See Context, p. 5.

43–6 A *gallery* (44) is a long room, often found in palaces or mansions, which adjoined the main room of the house. If the King were present, those wishing to see him would have to wait in the gallery. The image might be an allegory in which the soul waits to be called into God's presence or it could show life in England to be attractive in comparison with the moral squalor of the Continent.

47 Compare this with the last stanza of *Song: Sweetest love*.

51–4 How should this outburst be understood? Does it show he knows her so well he understands her fears, or does a phrase such as the *white Alps alone* (53) indicate he finds the prospect of travel exciting?

55 **Augur** forecast or predict.

except unless.

dread Jove God, but perhaps with a hint of the wilfulness and unpredictability associated with Greek and Roman gods.

Elegy 19: To his Mistress Going to Bed

This is a poem about anticipation. As the title states, it is about *Going to Bed* rather than what happens in it. Perhaps as a result of this, the poet's mind interestingly explores a wide range of ideas and associations. There is religious speculation, imagery about colonial adventures and an intellectually complex discourse on nakedness (see Interpretations, pp. 144-5). Is his mind more active than his hands? Readers are often surprised at how frank and detailed the poem is (think about all those layers of clothes). Yet is it a sensuously arousing piece (see Interpretations, p. 170)? And though the scene itself is detailed, there is much that we do not know. Is the woman his wife (perhaps this is her wedding-night), his mistress or a prostitute? Is it possible to imagine the events that led up to this encounter?

1 **Come** poems which are invitations to love often start with or emphasize this word.

my is the character of the poem indicated by the prominent use of the personal pronouns? Think about the rhyming of *my... defy... I... I... lie*. They might be read as assertively male or as sighs, as in sounds of the fourth stanza of *Song: Sweetest love*.

2 **labour... in labour lie**   the first *labour* means sexual activity, the second agonized anticipation.

3 **The foe**   military language was often used in love poems. Does it make the poem playful or emotionally antagonistic? The sexual joking in the poem might point to the former possibility, while the grammar (the poet gives orders) may lend support to the latter view.

4 **standing**   here, as in lines 11–12 and 23–4, the poet calls attention to his erect penis. Does this frankness create an erotic atmosphere or, given the unease about sustaining an erection (*tired*), is there the glimpse of an anxious lover, who suffers from self-doubt?

5 **girdle**   See Interpretations,   pp. 160-1.

5 **heaven's zone**   the Milky Way.

6 **a far fairer world**   the woman's body is seen as a *world*. Might this signify how wonderful she is, or that his desire is to discover, exploit and conquer?

7 **spangled breastplate**   ladies often wore jewelled stomachers, which covered their breasts.

9 **harmonious chime**   either the jingling of the jewels or her chiming watch.

11 **busk**   corset.

15 **wiry coronet**   a decorative band of metal worn round the brow.

16 **hairy diadem**   since diadems were associated with royalty, the implication may be that her natural beauty, in this case her hair, exceeds the beauty of her *coronet* (15) How important is this idea in the poem as a whole?

17–18   removing shoes is a religious act, performed when entering a holy place. Such language raises the issue of whether we are invited to view sexual union as a holy act. Consider Wilbur Sanders' view that this poem stands nearer to 'religion than all the conscious spirituality of *The Ecstasy*'.

21 **Mahomet's paradise**   Donne follows the uninformed popular view that Moslems imagined that in paradise there was endless sexual pleasure.

22 **Ill spirits walk in white**   Donne's contemporaries believed that it was often exceedingly difficult to tell a good from an evil spirit, because evil spirits were often disguised as good ones, that is, they appeared in angelic white. See note on 24.

23 **sprite** spirit.

24 **hairs... flesh** the idea here is that an erection enables the lover to distinguish between good and evil spirits. Some readers might find this a disappointing crudity; others might enjoy the wit of such a simple solution.

25 **License** allow, but possibly also the idea of taking out a licence for mining or other kinds of economic exploitation.

27 Different parts of America were described as new-found lands. See Context, p. 2 and Interpretations, p. 161 and p. 171.

29 **empery** empire.

30 **discovering** uncovering.

31 **bonds** her loving arms that will hold him fast, a legal agreement or, even, the *bonds* of indissoluble marriage.

32 **seal** this usually refers to the sexual organs, as in *The Relic* (29–30). The word also refers to the sealing of a legal document.

33 See Interpretations, p. 145.

34–5 Again, Donne uses religious language. The lover might feel a kind of religious wonder in the presence of his naked mistress, and he might also enjoy the oddity of comparing naked bodies to souls without bodies (see Interpretations, p. 140).

35–8 Donne alters the story of Hippomenes, who distracted Atalanta in a race by throwing golden balls in her way, by making Atalanta the one who distracted men by throwing down jewels. The lines leave it unclear as to who exactly is the fool.

40 **laymen** the idea here is that ordinary men (*laymen*) need pictures or fine bindings, whereas real scholars do not.

41–3 True lovers are like a small band of religious believers. Lovers only see their beloved's nakedness *revealed* if she grants them the privilege, and believers are only counted righteous (*imputed*) by God and are thus able to understand the revelations of the Bible (*mystic books*). (See Holy Sonnet 6, 13.) One of the critical issues of this poem is how we should take this conceit.

44 **midwife** is the word suitable? For a similar problem, see *The Flea* (8).

46 **penance... innocence** the implication is that although she wears white she might be neither penitent (those guilty of sexual crimes did public penance in white garments) nor innocent of sexual experience. Is the lover pleased she is not innocent?

48 **covering** the difficulty here is that this word was customarily
used of the copulation of horses and not people.

Holy Sonnet 6

In the octave of this sonnet (1–8) the poet creates in detail
the intense musings of a man anticipating his own death, and in the
cooler and more theological sestet (9–14) he attempts to calm
the fears aroused by the opening through the consoling hope of
imputed righteousness. Should we praise the octave's vivid
imagery and high emotional temperature, or be more impressed
by the intellectual clarity of the sestet, which is more humble and
self-aware than the octave's heated, theatrical rhetoric?

1–4 Might rapidly moving from one image to another show a
fascination with death, a fear so intense that he desperately
seeks to control it through a series of vivid and familiar images
or a dramatization of his plight to bring out how serious it is?
(See Interpretations, p. 152.)

5 **gluttonous death** a reader might recoil in horror from the
image of death as a predatory but otherwise hardly focused
creature, who will *instantly unjoint* (5) body and soul. But can we
exclude the grotesque humour of death as a glutton (*gluttonous*)
or a butcher (*unjoint*)?

7 **that face** what face? There are several answers: God, death,
the devil. Does this range of possible meanings enrich the
poem?

13 **Impute me righteous** this essentially Anglican (rather than
Roman Catholic) doctrine argues that as Adam's sin, due to the
fall, is attributed, or imputed, to all, salvation is only possible
if people are correspondingly imputed righteous by the merits
of Christ's suffering and death upon the cross. The sermon in
the *Second Book of Homilies* (1563) on justification contains this
remark: 'we cannot be accounted righteous, but by Christ's
merits imputed to us'.

14 **For thus I leave** the significance of the theatrical close (it is

like an actor's dramatic exit) depends upon whether the poet confidently departs, knowing he has been imputed righteous. If, however, it is an histrionic (the gesture of an actor) movement, the reader might see just how in need of mercy this self-regarding poet is.

The words *the world, the flesh, and devil* are a reference to the Baptism Service in *The Book of Common Prayer*. They might indicate that, as at baptism, the sins have been renounced or that he draws attention to his still fallen state to strengthen his plea for mercy.

Holy Sonnet 7

There are striking contrasts between the octave and the sestet (see Interpretations, p. 166). The opening is colourful, highly peopled and even theatrical, whereas what follows is visually spare and highly individualistic. The tone changes from bold gestures (it is as if he, rather than God, announces the Last Judgement) to low-key requests that God teaches him how to repent.

1 **round earth's imagined corners**   The image combines the roundness of the earth with words from the last book of the Bible: *four angels standing at the four corners of the earth* (Revelation 7.1). Perhaps the deliberate strangeness of the language is appropriate to an event so unparalleled that words have to be stretched and extended beyond their ordinary meanings in order to imagine it.

4 **to your scattered bodies go**   at the last Judgement souls will be reunited with their bodies. (See Interpretations, p. 152.)

5 **flood... fire**   *flood* refers to Genesis 6–8 (the first book in the Bible) and *fire* to Revelation 8. What does this time span from beginning to end contribute to the poem?

6 **agues**   diseases.

9 **But let them sleep, Lord**   These words create a problem typical of Donne's religious verse. Is this impudent blasphemy,

> or the uncertain humour of a man aware of the gulf between him and Christ?
>
> 10 **abound** in Romans 5:20 St Paul writes: 'where sin abounded, there grace abounded much more'.
>
> 12 **there; here** does this simple placing together enhance or detract from the gravity of the sonnet?
>
> 13–14 The tone here is difficult. The almost colloquial *for that's as good* might indicate either confidence or nervous bluster. Likewise, Christian doctrine asserts that Christ has sealed everybody's pardon with the blood of the cross, yet the effect of *As if* might make the final line sound more tentative (see Interpretations, pp. 150-1).

Holy Sonnet 10

This sonnet may be read as a poetic duel with death, in which word-play corresponds to skilful swordsmanship, and variations in pace and emotional intensity to the thrusts and parries of the poet's attack and defence. (The last sermon Donne preached to the court of King Charles I was called *Death's Duel*.) It is difficult to characterize the overall tone: is he serious in the face of a mighty foe, cosily intimate and even casually witty at death's expense or denigrating almost to the extent of being sneering? Another problem is that the argument is clearly false, being based on analogies such as the conventional one between sleep and death. It might be said in defence that the poem tackles not death but the language we use of it – *though some have called thee/Mighty and dreadful* (1–2). Perhaps we value the poem not for its argument but the convincing creation of an anxious mind bracing itself against death with a variety of images.

> 1 **proud** the word has the sense of being outstanding and awe-inspiring as well as boastfully self-confident. Both senses are also present in *swell'st* (12).
>
> 4 **nor yet canst thou kill me** the quickened pace of these heavily stressed monosyllables might suggest a lively confidence

that the poet has the measure of his opponent, or they could be a defensive thrust at a strong adversary, whom he fears.

8 **delivery**   the soul is delivered in the sense that at death it is born into eternity and so delivered from the prison of life.

9 See Interpretations, p. 148.

13 **wake eternally**   wake to the presence of God. Is there a quiet confidence in the restraint of such language that is more appealing and religiously profound than the direct appeals of, for instance, *Holy Sonnet 14*?

14 **Death thou shalt die**   is this an effective end to the poem? Is it inconsistent to write off the fear of death only to serve it up as a threat to Death itself? A defence might be that to die is to pass to a realm, where Death is no more.

Holy Sonnet 13

The tension, as in so many Donne poems, is between divine and earthly love. In the intensely realized presentation of the crucified Christ, Donne may be, as elsewhere, dependent upon traditions of religious meditation in which those who prayed pictured in their imaginations scenes from the Bible (see Context, p. 12). By contrast, the sestet is relaxed and even casual; we might imagine the poet confidently shaking his head in *No, no; but as in my idolatry* (9). As with most of the sonnets, it is important to see how the close settles the intellectual and emotional energies. For a discussion of the form of the sonnet, see Interpretations, p. 166.

1 See Interpretations, p. 156.

2 **Mark**   the word had contemplative and meditative connotations.

4 **countenance**   in the Bible this word is frequently used of God's face: 'The Lord lift up his countenance upon thee' (Numbers 6:26). Think about how Donne writes about the face of God and the face of his beloveds.

5 **amazing**   frightening or even horrifying.

6 **pierced head**   see St Mark 15:17: '*and platted a crown of thorns and put it about his head*'.

8 **forgiveness** see St Luke's account of the crucifixion: 'Jesus said, Father, forgive them; for they know not what they do' (23:34) .

10 **profane mistresses** he worshipped women as if they were divine. Does the argument of the sonnet depend upon a contrast or a comparison between Christ and his *profane mistresses*? See Interpretations, p. 149 and p. 175.

11–12 the idea is that only ugly women have no pity on ardent lovers.

14 **This beauteous form** Christ is both beautiful and full of pity. How far is the beauty of Christ from the beauty of his *profane mistresses* (10)?

Holy Sonnet 14

Nowhere else in Donne's religious poetry is the drama and the contradictory violence of paradox so evident as in this sonnet (see Interpretations, p. 152.). There is something thrilling, even exhilarating, about the lightness and speed of the poet's thought and the way the paradoxes mount to the breathtaking and outrageous climax of the closing couplet. Is Donne attempting to renew a jaded religious language? Is the poem in danger of delighting in contradictions?

1 **my... you** as in many of the love poems, the frequency and impact of the first and second person pronouns is important.

2,4 The lines contrast *Break, blow, burn* (4) with *knock, breathe, shine* (2). Some of the words have strong biblical associations. Christ in Revelation 3:20 says: 'Behold I stand at the door and knock', and in St Matthew 6:19 it is 'thieves who break through and steal'.

5 **usurped town** a town in which power has illegally (and probably violently) passed from a legitimate ruler to an invader.
another it is not clear who or what *another* is; it could be the devil, death, sin, doubt, despair or a human lover.

7 **viceroy** one who wields power on behalf of a supreme (and usually absent) ruler.

8 See Interpretations, p. 150.

9 **fain**   willingly or gladly. See Interpretations p. 175.

11 **Divorce**   this word is central to an implied story, which acts as a parallel to the poet's religious state: a woman has desperately fallen in love (9) but is betrothed, married or has been stolen by another so cannot be *free* (13) or *chaste* (14) (the word was applied to married couples) until her true love divorces her from the one to whom she is bound. But the idea is hardly Christian. The Anglican marriage service insists: 'Those whom God hath joined together let no man put asunder.' Can the word *divorce* ever be appropriately used of God's relationships with his people?

Holy Sonnet 17

This is a poem of strong feelings, which the poet hardly seems to fully understand. Perhaps its expression of uncertainty is what makes it successful. Is it, for example, about human or divine love? It also seems unfinished. Lines 9–14 set out God's attitude to the poet (9–14), but no response is given.

Donne's biography may be relevant here. His wife, Ann Donne, died on 15 August 1617, seven days after giving birth to their twelfth child. She was 33. The poem might not have been written immediately afterwards; Helen Gardner thinks that it might date from 1619.

1–4 The logical use of *Since* and the conventional characterization of death as paying a *debt/To nature* might suggest that the poet accepts his loss with little or no anguish. But the heavy stresses at the end of the first line and the way the rhythm singles out the painful word *early* (3) could indicate a deeply-felt grief.

3 **ravished**   carried away into heaven.

4 **Wholly**   is there a pun on holy?

5 **whet**   sharpen and make ready.

6 **seek thee God**   try to hear how the cadence leads to the word God. Are there stronger climaxes in the poem?

8 **A holy thirsty dropsy melts me**   the language is poised
between divine and earthly love. The words *thirsty* and *dropsy*
apply to both, though *melts* (emotionally affects) is more
appropriate to love poetry (see Context, p. 5).

9–10 God is cast in the role of a father who supplies the dowry of
Christ's love (*offering all thine*) to bring about the heavenly
marriage of the poet and his dead beloved.

13 **tender jealousy**   God is presented in the Bible as jealous; that
is, as holding on to what is rightly his. What does *tender* add to
this idea? See *A Hymn to Christ, at the Author's last going into
Germany*, 20.
doubt   fear and suspect.

Holy Sonnet 19

Instead of images of the Last Judgement, the figure of Death or the
crucified Christ, the poet, through rapid changes in tone, pace and
cadence, expresses puzzlement at his own spiritual state. Does this
narrower range make it less impressive than other *Holy Sonnets*?
The phrase *contraries meet in one* is a good description of the
tensions of the poem as well as of the spiritual state of the poet.
See Interpretations, p. 149.

1 **vex**   the word had a much stronger meaning in the seventeenth
century than it has today, being closer to shaken with anguish.

2–3 **Inconstancy/constant**   what is the effect of this verbal playing
upon the poet's distress?

4 **vows**   the relationship between religious poetry and love
poetry which emerges in some of the *Holy Sonnets* is present in
this and other words in the poem.

5 **humorous**   changeable.
Contrition   being sorry for one's sins.

7 **riddlingly distempered**   his contrition wildly swings from one
extreme to another as if he were unbalanced by disease.

9 **I durst**   unlike some of the other *Holy Sonnets*, there is not a
sharp break between the octave and the sestet. Does this make
it an impressively concentrated poem, or do you miss the

drama of a change from one mood to another?

11 **rod**   God's justice and punishment are frequently spoken of as a rod.

13 **fantastic**   uncertain, extreme, unpredictable.
   ague   a disease or fever.

13–14 Does the paradox of his *best days* (a phrase often used when talking about health) being those when he *shake(s) with fear* successfully sum up the *contraries* (1) of the poem?

Good Friday, 1613. Riding Westward

This poem, which opens with intellectual speculation and closes with an ardent plea that God will redeem him, typically blends a poetic realization that his westward journey accurately mirrors the state of his relationship to God with an anguished realization of how serious that relationship is. In keeping with the poetic or fabricated nature of the poem, what is seen is the product not of the physical eye but of the imagination. In line 33 he says that the Cross of Christ is far *from mine eye*, and in line 35 there is a telling picture of the guilty poet with his back to Christ yet his memory fixed on him.

1–10 Donne works with the astronomical theory that each planet consisted of a sphere controlled by an intelligence or spirit. Planets could come under the influence of another more powerful agent and so be governed by it rather than following their natural course – (*natural form*) (6). The natural direction was from west to east, but so powerful was the Primum Mobile (in Donne's analogy the *first mover*, line 8) that they actually travelled in the reverse direction (see Context, p. 7).

8 **whirled**   there might be a pun here.

11 **sun**   another pun?
   rising   *rising* could mean the incarnation of Christ, the physical lifting up of the cross or the resurrection.

13 **But that**   except that.

17 This is a common Biblical idea: *Thou canst not see my face: for*

there shall no man see me and live (Exodus 33:20).

19–20 The New Testament says that the crucifixion of Jesus was accompanied by darkness – 'darkness over all the land' (St Matthew 27:45), and that at his death there was an earthquake – 'and the earth did shake, and the stones were cloven' (St Matthew 27:51). The word *lieutenant* is Donne's own metaphor for nature as God's second in command; *footstool* is a Biblical metaphor for the earth being under God's authority – 'the earth is my footstool' (Isaiah 66:1). See Interpretations p. 151.

24 **Zenith... antipodes** wherever one is on earth (*antipodes* means its furthest points), God is an absolute distance from us.

25–6 Some believed that souls had their seat or basis in blood, though theologians questioned whether this could apply to Christ (*if not of his*). They agreed, however, that since salvation came through the cross, all souls rested in Christ's blood.

29–32 There is an ancient practice of contemplating the figure of Mary, the Mother of Jesus, at the foot of the cross. Mary was God's partner, because she agreed to bear the Christ child, and thus she provided *Half of that sacrifice* by which the world was redeemed (*ransomed*).

36 **tree** the cross.

37 **but** only.

38 **Corrections** punishments aimed at reforming him.
   leave stop.

39–40 Compare the violence of these pleas (demands?) with the language of *Holy Sonnet 14* (1–4). How strong in both is the idea that the poet would rather be the object of God's anger than be ignored?

41 **Restore thine image** salvation was thought of as a return to mankind's original estate, when the image of God was clearly present in people.

A Hymn to Christ, at the Author's last going into Germany

In this grave poem, the poet examines his spiritual state. We hear him meditating on its seriousness in the strong monosyllabic thrust of many of the words. Through a consideration of such weighty issues as death, providence, and the nature of love, he moves towards a climactic decision. Because there are many ideas and the pace is fast, readers will need to take their time with it.

Title On 12 May 1619 Donne sailed as chaplain with the Earl of Doncaster's diplomatic mission to the German Princes. Shortly before he left he preached a farewell sermon at Lincoln's Inn in which he spoke of Christ and the sea: *Sea of his blood.*

2 **my emblem of thy ark** an emblem was a visual representation of a quality or idea in a system of thought; it was usually used as a teaching device and was often accompanied by a woodcut and a short poem giving a moral comment. Here the poet makes a traditional association between a ship and Noah's ark, which survived the Flood. The ark is emblematic of Divine providence and the Church.

4 **blood** the word *blood* stands for the redemption of mankind by the cross of Christ.

8 **never** is the emphatic stress on *never* one of unswerving conviction, or is there an element of bravado in it, possibly arising from doubt or fear?

9 **sacrifice** the word *sacrifice* includes the idea that he renounces his earthly and temporal loves and that he gives them, or offers them, to God.
    Island England.

12 **thy sea** see note on line 4.

14 **winter** the word suggests age, the loss of earthly pleasure and the absence of his own inner, or spiritual, resources. Thus, in a line that effectively says he is nothing, Donne characteristically plays on the multiple meanings of a word.

17 **control** in a soul which is whole and integrated (*harmonious*) there is no need for Christ or the Church to check or restrain (*control*) its love.

18 **amorousness** this word might suggest earthly and even erotic love rather than the love the soul has for God. As with many of Donne's poems, we might ask whether there is a struggle over the renunciation of earthly ties or a similarity between sexual love and the love of God.

20 **jealous**   the idea that God possessively loves and guards all that belongs to him frequently occurs in the Bible: 'for I am the Lord, thy God, a jealous God' (Exodus 20:5). Here Christ is the jealous lover.

21–2 See *Holy Sonnet* 17 (9–10).

22 **who ever gives, takes liberty**   this can mean both that giving one's love is not always justified (that is, one takes a liberty in doing so) and that whoever gives someone love takes away that person's freedom.

23–4 See Interpretations, p. 151.

25 **divorce**   see note on *Holy Sonnet* 14 (11).

26 **fainter beams**   the beams of the sun are often symbols of God's or Christ's (there is a pun on son) love for the world.

28 **hopes**   worldly prospects such as a place in the life of the court.

29 Consider the place in this and other religious poems of how negation – lack of light, lack of love, lack of success – is the way to God. To what extent in Donne is it the absence of things (even the absence of religious experience) that brings the poet to God?

30 **I go out of sight**   this could mean 'I travel far away' and 'I die'.

32 Does the dark and long falling cadence close the poem heavily and gloomily, or is there a distinctive triumph in that the poet has freely chosen *night* rather than worldly pleasures (28), knowing it will bring him to God?

Hymn to God my God, in my Sickness

Perhaps the most remarkable aspect of this poem is its serene tone. There is no apparent anguish, and, unlike some of the Holy Sonnets, the many paradoxes and polarities (for instance: *do/think* (5), *west/east* (13), *death/resurrection* (15)) are not born out of spiritual turmoil, and, what is more, they are neatly resolved. Such neatness makes the poem intellectually elegant; to use a metaphor from the poem itself, everything is mapped out with a satisfying clarity. Even the potential violence of the last line could be allayed by seeing that the idea is not a sudden dramatic outburst but a text carefully chosen by the preacher in which *throws down* is balanced by the religiously important word *raise*. Perhaps the poem captures the experience that many sick or dying people have of being happily released from the body's pain and free to view themselves in a detached and spiritually calm way.

Title Isaac Walton claimed that the poem was written during
       Donne's final illness in 1631, but it may have been composed
       during or shortly after a serious illness he suffered in 1623.

1 **holy room** heaven.

4 **I tune the instrument** a musician, being only an employee,
   would tune his instrument before entering the banqueting hall
   of a mansion. The image might mean prepare oneself with
   prayers before death or practise the art of poetry so that the
   harmony of verse may anticipate the harmony of the *choir of
   saints* (2).

5 **before** this word draws attention to how the opening stanza is
   separated from the others: how should the relation between it
   and the rest of the poem be understood? Does the musical
   imagery successfully prepare us for the emotionally composed
   and serene tone of the poem, or is the jump from a domestic
   setting to the furthest parts of the world so extreme as to cut
   this stanza off damagingly from the rest?

6 **love** the doctors' loving concern for him.

7 **Cosmographers... map** because, according to a common
   contemporary idea, a person was a little world, it is poetically
   appropriate to see his physicians as geographers (*cosmographers*)
   examining a *map* of the world (see Context, p. 3).

9 **my south-west discovery** a *discovery* was a passage or route
   into distant parts of the world. Here the geographical image
   functions figuratively: south is the region of heat and west is
   where the sun sets; that is to say, he expects to die as the result
   of a fever. See Context, p. 2.

10 **Per fretum febris** this means both 'through the raging fever'
   and 'through the strait of fever'.
   straits this can mean a narrow passage of sea water, the trials
   and difficulties of life and the hard way to salvation.

11 **I joy** is the poet fully aware of his plight and yet able to
rejoice at the prospect of death, or is he only confident because
he has avoided the reality of death by, so to speak, disguising it
in elegant and intellectually clever imagery? See Interpretations,
p. 154.

13–14 Donne makes this point in one of his sermons: 'but to paste
that flat Map upon a round body, and then West and East are
all one'. In theological terms *west* is death and *east* symbolizes
the resurrection. See note on lines 10–13 in *A Valediction: of
Weeping*.

16–17 There was a centuries-old debate about the geographical
location of Eden, the earthly paradise. As Eden was a mirror
of Heaven, the images and emblems of these lines are all
associated with Paradise. *Pacific* means peaceful; *Jerusalem*, as
well as being an image of the heavenly city, also means vision
of peace, and *eastern riches* is reminiscent of the imagery in the
Gospels for the Kingdom of Heaven – treasure and great
pearls.

18 The *Anyan* straits were supposed to separate North America
from Asia. The straits of *Magellan* are at the foot of South
America, and the Mediterranean Sea is entered through the
straits of *Gibraltar*.

20 It was traditionally believed that after the Biblical flood the
world was divided between the sons of Noah: Japheth (*Japhet*)
was given Europe, Ham (*Cham*) Africa and *Shem* Asia.

21–2 The conceit of the map leads to the much debated issue of
where Paradise was located (16–17). Donne explores the
widespread belief that since Eden was in the region of
Mesopotamia, it was in the same location (*stood in one place*) as
Jerusalem, where Christ was crucified. There are also legends
about how the wood for Christ's cross came from a tree that
grew out of the bones of Adam. St Paul compares Adam to
Christ; for instance: 'For as in Adam all die, even so in Christ
shall all be made alive' (I Corinthians 15:22). Christ is also the
'last Adam' (I Corinthians 15:45).

24 **sweat** because Adam brought death into the world through
the fall, the poet's feverish sweat is that of the first Adam.

25 **blood** see note on *A Hymn to Christ, at the Author's last going
into Germany* (4).

26 **purple**   the conceit is that Christ's blood is like a robe of royal purple.

27 **thorns... other crown**   thorns could mean the crown of thorns which Christ wore when he brought about salvation on the cross, and the poet might figuratively be referring to his own sufferings as being like a crown of thorns. The *other crown* is the heavenly crown worn by those in heaven.

29 **to mine own**   to myself. See Interpretations, p. 162.

30 Strictly speaking this is not a Biblical text. Nevertheless, it reflects Biblical thinking in its paradox that those who are raised are those that have been thrown down.

A Hymn to God the Father

Walton records that this poem was written during Donne's illness of 1623. Its tone, imagery, argument and manner may, therefore, be usefully compared to *Hymn to God my God, in my Sickness*, which may have been written at the same time. The movement and tone are memorable: its pace is measured, and in the gravity and honesty of its brooding self-questioning there is a dark yet dignified progress towards the final plea and the undemonstrative assurance of the close. The big problem of the poem is whether the tone is consistently maintained. Is this a poem in which the mind of the poet is concentrated with moving seriousness upon his relationship with God, or is he, at points, preoccupied with his own skill as a poet, who exploits the possibilities of language? See Interpretations, p. 161.

Title   Why is the poem addressed to God the Father? In the closing stanza there is a pun on Christ as the Son of God and the sun: should the poem be read as being about the salvation brought by the Son of God, or should it be interpreted as the humble request of a man who wants God the Father to accept him as a son? Can it be both?

1–12   There are four questions in the first two stanzas; if you try reading them aloud you may notice that, unusually, the final cadence falls rather than rises (see Interpretations, p. 158). What is the effect of this? Does it suggest that the poet is assured of salvation so the question is not a real one or, conversely, that he is so absorbed in meditating upon his unworthiness that he dare not question God in an ordinary way?

1 **begun**   according to Christian doctrine, humanity is marked by the fall of Adam (Genesis 3) and thus bears his guilt. This is called original sin. It was sometimes thought of as being transmitted from one generation to another through procreation. Hence when he *begun* he was a sinner.

5 **done**   should a man who is so aware of his need for God's mercy allow himself the poetic indulgence of a pun on his own name? Is the introduction of the pun a flaw, because it detracts from the weighty seriousness of the poem's tone? It might be argued that it is a daring and successful way of showing how delightful it would be to be possessed and owned by God. See Interpretations, p. 161.

6 **more**   some critics detect a pun on Donne's wife's name – Ann More.

7 **that sin**   the sin could be any wrong deed that led others astray, and, more specifically, the writing of sexually explicit poetry.

10 **wallowed**   this could be a comic moment of self-mockery, in which he pictures himself grotesquely indulging in sin. Another possibility is that as there is a traditional association between wallowing and pigs, the poet is imagining himself in the role of the prodigal son (St Luke 15:11–32), who, in his poverty, was forced to mind pigs before he came to his senses and returned to his father.

13 **fear**   the fear is that he might not be saved. To despair of the possibility of one's own salvation was considered the worst spiritual state into which one could fall.

14 **thread**   life was sometimes pictured as a thread spun out and finally cut by the Fates; here, however, the poet spins his own life and is, consequently, solely responsible for all his wrongdoing.
perish   it is perhaps significant that in the Authorized Version of the Bible this word appears in the story of the prodigal son: 'and I perish with hunger! I will arise and go to my father' (St Luke 15:17–18).

shore which way does this image work? Is he the drowning sailor who dies just as he reaches the shore, or is the sea a symbol of God, which the poet fails to attain because he dies on the shore?

16 **shine... shines** Donne may be thinking of the words of Jesus: 'he [God] maketh his sun to rise on the evil and on the good' (St Matthew 5:45).

17 **thou hast done** if the pun works, this is its triumphant resolution: the work of Christ is completed and Donne's salvation is secured because God takes him as his own.

Interpretations

Interpretations through subject matter

Striking and ambivalent

Donne's poetry is like flashes of light in a dark room. The reader is often surprised and delighted by the striking originality of the poet's thinking. Moreover, the flashes of light are not always of the same kind. In a single poem, Donne can open up several distinct areas of thought. His is a poetry of *things/Extreme, and scatt'ring bright (Air and Angels*, line 21–2).

Donne's thinking is also ambivalent. The reader is often unclear as to what the tone of the poem is. This makes interpretation a challenge. Is his subject matter sacred or profane? Is he a poet of reason or feeling? Is he more at home with ideas than with people? Does he play the role of the adventurous lover Jack Donne or Dr Donne the preacher? Is he in control of his poems or distracted by the turmoil of his own language?

Faced with poems that zigzag in their thought and are ambivalent in their attitudes, it is not easy to sum up their subject matter. We should never forget that the ideas exist alongside each other within single poems. A frequent example of this is souls and bodies.

Souls and bodies

When Donne writes about the soul, his language sounds rarefied. In *The Ecstasy* he imagines one *so by love refined,/That he soul's language understood* (21–2). It is quite easy to believe that if a soul could speak, it would do so in Donne's airy, insubstantial sound textures. Listen to the echoed vowels in *so* and *soul's* and in *by* and *refined*. Donne might be implicitly claiming that he is the one who understands *soul's language*.

But, of course, Donne knows there are problems with making such a claim. How can a soul speak and act without a body? He turns to this teasing question at the close of *The Ecstasy*:

> Love's mysteries in souls do grow,
> But yet the body is his book. (71–2)

These lines have a philosophical clarity. Love grows in the soul and is displayed in the body. The body, therefore, is an instrument of revelation; we can read it like a book.

The tensions of body and soul

The life of many Donne poems is found in the tensions between the impulses of the body and the aspirations of the soul. Four things may be said about these tensions.

- Donne is sometimes attracted by the idea that the soul cannot change. Writing in *The Ecstasy* about the new being created out of the lovers' two souls, he says that it is *composed* of souls, *whom no change can invade* (46–8). In a world in which all things change, the idea of an unchanging soul is comforting and attractive.

- Hence the idea of leaving the body is desirable. The most extraordinary expression of this is in *Elegy 19*, which argues: *As souls unbodied, bodies unclothed must be* (34). This is close to suggesting that as nakedness is our natural state, so is the soul without the body.

- Yet Donne can urge a return to the body: *To our bodies turn we then* (*The Ecstasy*, line 69). As is said in *Air and Angels*, without a body the soul could *nothing do* (8).

- On a philosophical level, there is a reversal of Plato's ideas (see Context, pp. 12-13). Plato sought the Ideal Forms in and through particular things, whereas Donne is closer to Blake in wanting to see 'the human form divine' (Blake: *The Divine Image*, line 11). In both *Air and Angels* and *The Good Morrow*, he wants the fleeting glimpses of female perfection to be fully present in a particular woman's *lip, eye, and brow (Air and Angels,* line 14).

Love and the body

There has been much debate about the full significance of *To our bodies turn we then (The Ecstasy,* line 69). The meaning might be that souls live in and through their bodies, or it could be an invitation to the act of love. Certainly, there can be no act of love without a body to do the acting.

Donne is not a visual poet, so perhaps the physical details of the human body that do occur in the poems have greater significance. One of the pleasures of reading Donne, we should remember, is imagining those essentially dramatic situations in which the poet gazes at his beloved. *A Valediction: forbidding Mourning* is about restraining the emotions aroused by parting, and yet, even when he says their love does not require the physical presence of the other, he allows himself to dwell lingeringly and lovingly upon her face, claiming that refined lovers such as they are *Care less, eyes, lips, and hands to miss* (20). If, as in drama, we imagine him touching the features he singles out, we may wonder whether he really cares any *less* than lovers *Whose soul is sense* (14).

Donne the lover

Donne the lover is the figure (or figures) created in the poems. When writing about him, we should always remember that we cannot directly connect the poems with Donne's life, because it is not known when most of them were written. In any case, even if we could, it would not follow that the poems are about Donne's experiences of love. A poet who can imagine a woman's viewpoint in *Break of Day* is also capable of imagining men in love. Donne's poetry certainly feels like the fruits of raw experience, but art can convey what a raw experience is like without the artist having undergone it.

The experiences in the poems are remarkably varied in their tones, emotions and the roles the poet plays.

- There are love poems in which body and soul are united. Poems such as *The Anniversary, The Canonization, The Good Morrow* and *The Sun Rising* are physically and intellectually exuberant. Their imagery is celebratory: lovers are kings (or better than kings), and love is so pure that it cannot die. In *The Sun Rising* the poet relishes his role of the one who feels that in possessing his beloved, he possesses all things.

- The soul – *loveliness within (The Undertaking*, line 13) – is sometimes the sole object of love. *The Relic* celebrates a love that never goes beyond a kiss.

- Sometimes, as in *The Expiration* and *Song: Sweetest love*, the poems are about parting and absence. The reason for absence is often a journey, but the imagery of death, or possible death, is prominent. The feelings in the parting poems are often exceptionally strong and raise the issue of the importance of the body to lovers.

- Sometimes what interests the poet is the nature of love itself. In *The Ecstasy, Lovers' Infiniteness* and *Love's Growth* the wonder of love prompts philosophical reflection on what the word 'love' means. In *Love's Growth* the poet tries to make sense of the high-flown language he once used of love. How, he asks, can I have said that *My love was infinite, if spring hath made it more* (6).

- Donne does not ignore the power struggles of love. *The Flea* can be read as a strategy for seduction in which the poet is ardent and intellectually able. In *The Dream* the poet is increasingly insistent upon the woman complying, and *Break of Day*, written from the woman's viewpoint, adopts a series of arguments to persuade the man to stay.

- It is perhaps not surprising that Donne should write about rejection, as the poem of unrequited (unreturned) love was popular in his day and both before and since. *Twicknam Garden* is interesting, because rejection, as in the case of success in love, prompts him to ingenious thoughts. Lovers, he suggests, can test the sincerity of their beloveds' tears by comparing them with his.

- At least one poem – *Love's Alchemy* – is aggressively cynical. Its rough manner and grating verbal music reveal a hostility to women and to all those who make high claims for love.

- Perhaps some poems are more extreme. *The Apparition* is spiteful in that the poet enjoys anticipating the fear and horror of his *murderess* (1). The poet also appears to take pleasure in the barrage of questions and arguments fired at the entirely silent woman in *Woman's Constancy*.

- An aspect of Donne that might disturb the reader is the desire of the poet in the poem to exert control. To put it simply: the poet does all the talking. Readers might feel that a psychological interpretation is needed here. Does the need to assert intellectual authority conceal a fear of failure in love?

- Two poems – *A Nocturnal upon S. Lucy's Day, being the shortest day* and *A Fever* – deal with devastating loss or the threat of loss. It is worth asking whether *A Nocturnal* is more deeply felt than the exuberant poems.

Activity

The above points sketch out a 'map' of Donne's love poetry. Look through the selection to see if you can make it more detailed and perhaps locate features not mentioned above.

Discussion

You may have found poems that work as opposing pairs. Is, for instance, *The Good Morrow* a palinode (a poem written to reverse what was said in another poem) of *Love's Alchemy*? (It could, of course, be the other way round.) What do you make of *The Funeral* or *The Triple Fool*? You may be left wondering whether Donne is essentially a poet of the joys or the disappointments of love. Finally, it is important to remember that there is no evidence that Donne had a pre-conceived plan to write particular kinds of poems.

Nakedness

In Donne's day (and before) the naked body did not have an unambiguously erotic status. Many visual representations of nakedness were associated with death, poverty and shame. In pictures of the Last Judgement (the subject of *Holy Sonnet 7*) scrawny naked forms emerge from the earth to appear before the Judgement seat of God. It was customary to place a naked, decomposing body on the tombs of Lords and Bishops to remind everyone that even great ones come to dust. Even a contemporary poet noted for the sensuousness of his writing, Christopher Marlowe, uses a phrase suggestive of blunt exposure and perhaps vulnerability – *stark naked (Elegy 1)*.

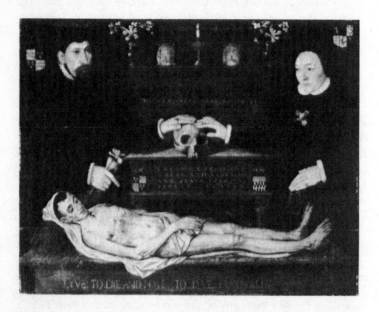

The Judd Memorial. Pictures that reminded people of the inevitability of death were common in Donne's day, particularly on tombs and memorials.

Donne's attitudes to nakedness may have been shaped by this essentially late medieval outlook. Is there a recoil from the flesh in the sweat of *The Apparition*? Yet Donne can surprise us. Take the line: *Full nakedness, all joys are due to thee (Elegy 19: To his Mistress Going to Bed*, line 33). This expression of delight suggests that nakedness is the full and proper state. A body when naked does not lack anything and nor is it, as *stark naked* suggests, disturbing and somehow unnatural in its exposure. By contrast, the words *full nakedness* point to a state that is satisfyingly complete with, of course, the reminder of our original and ideal condition. In the light of that original condition – the story of the Garden of Eden (Genesis 3) – talk about nakedness as full and achieved is fitting and appropriate. Line 34 argues that as the true state of the soul is without a body, so the true state of the body is to be naked. Only naked bodies can *taste whole joys* (35).

Different views of the body

In the love poems, the beloved is placed very close to the lover / poet. In *The Good Morrow*, the lover lies so close to his beloved that he can see his reflection in her face: *My face in thine eye, thine in mine appears* (15). As the face mirrors the mind, the image confirms a mutual indwelling of soul with soul.

Yet, as always, Donne also adopts other stances. There are poems in which the body is viewed from a distance and, sometimes, coldly. The distance can be one of time. In *The Funeral* and *The Relic*, the poet imagines a future in which he is dead. The blunt, matter-of-fact tone of *The Damp* shows him imagining his own autopsy.

In such different views of the body we might see the spirit of intellectual inquiry (see Context, pp. 5-6) at odds with the impulses of the love poet. One of the features of Donne that readers have to cope with is the co-existence of loving intimacy and the more distant view of the Renaissance intellectual.

Death and burial

C.A. Patrides, having noted that Donne is known as a love poet, insists that death was also his subject: 'Death was for Donne an obsession'. Patrides eloquently adds that though his love of love altered, 'his love of death was undeviating, constant, permanent, fixed'. The famous image of Donne wrapped in his shroud for burial (see the picture on page 147) was made at his insistence while he was alive.

The poetic language of the day linked love and death: sexual consummation was described as a death (*The Damp*, 21) as was also breaking off a kiss (*The Expiration*, 1–2). Another convention was that parting from a beloved was death. Significantly, *A Valediction: forbidding Mourning* opens with a death-bed scene (see Context, p. 15).

Activity

To what extent is *Song: Sweetest love* a poem about death?

Discussion

It may be that Donne is doing more than repeat the poetic convention that parting from a beloved is like death. Is he only using himself in jest when, in the first stanza, he treats parting as a preparation for death? The possibility of an actual death dominates the poem. The last three stanzas imagine some terrible disaster. In the final stanza he fears that her premonitions will be fulfilled by fate (*destiny*). Perhaps even in the last simple, domestic detail of the couple turning aside to sleep, there is the shadow of sleep as an image of death.

Donne dwells on the details of burial. *Whoever comes to shroud me*, he says at the opening of *The Funeral*. (Most bodies were wrapped in shrouds rather than placed in coffins.) *The Relic* may be a continuation of *The Funeral*. Here the poet pictures his grave being opened up, as was the custom, to receive a second burial. Perhaps the most surprising mention of burial occurs in

John Donne in a shroud. This engraving appeared in *Death's Duel*, a sermon of Donne's published in 1632. Perhaps it looks as if he is meditating seriously rather than reposing in the sleep of death.

The Anniversary. The first stanza is a triumphant celebration of a love that defies the passage of time (*Only our love hath no decay*, line 7), but the second opens on a sobering note: *Two graves must hide thine and my corse*. The imagination that we find in Donne's poems is one that includes the certainty of death in even its most joyful poems.

Death is a presence in many of the religious poems. Again, it is Patrides who points to the way disturbances in rhythm call attention to the forces that rule our lives. In the confident and almost intimate address to death in *Holy Sonnet 10*, three uncontrollable agents – *fate, chance, kings* – disrupt the flow of the line: *Thou art slave to fate, chance, kings, and desperate men* (9).

The perspective of time

The Last Judgement is the theme of *Holy Sonnets, 6, 7* and *13*, and preparing to meet God face to face is the substance of the two *Hymns*. Donne is, as D.W. Harding argued, a poet of anticipation. Harding had in mind events not too far off, but the idea applies equally to a more distant future. Donne builds into his poems the perspective of what, in *Holy Sonnet 7*, he sums up as *When we are there* (12).

This concern to see events from the future also characterizes the love poems. Donne often speaks with the authority of one who knows what the future will be like. In *The Canonization* he confidently says that he and his beloved will be honoured in the future for embodying *peace* rather than the *rage* people of the then present find (39).

We might ask whether this interest in the future is a working out of the idea of the Last Judgement. The Last Judgement is seen as full and final. Does Donne imagine future events in a similar way? *The Canonization* and *The Relic* anticipate a future recognition of how remarkable Donne and his beloved were. In a very different emotional key *The Apparition* anticipates a successful posthumous revenge. With the hard gaze of posterity, the ghost of the lover judges the fearful woman as faithless.

These poems express no doubt that this is what the future will be.

Sacred and profane

Sacred means whatever is holy. *The Holy Sonnets* deal with the soul's longing for God, the desire to live a good life, the ever-present reality of God's judgement and, as noted above, the certainty of death. Profane means whatever lies outside the realm of the sacred – the worldly, the secular. Though Donne wrote poems that we might individually call sacred and profane, there is sometimes much in common between them. In two poems the link is explicitly made. *Holy Sonnet 19* is a troubled meditation on *inconstancy* (2) in which the language of wooing is used of religious devotion – *I court God* (10). In *Holy Sonnet 13* he compares what he is about to say to God with what he said to his mistresses:

> **but as in my idolatry**
> **I said to all my profane mistresses** (9–10)

If sacred and profane had nothing in common, he could not compare speaking to God with speaking to a mistress.

There are many other moments when the sacred and the profane meet.

- Donne builds on a Petrarchan convention that saw love as a kind of religion. Hence, in *A Valediction: forbidding Mourning* ordinary people are called the *laity* (8), and in *The Undertaking* those incapable of the high love the poet claims to have achieved are called *profane* (22).
- Donne uses religious thinking in his love poems. In *The Dream*, he clearly implies that his beloved, whom he first mistook for an angel, actually knows him as does God. He wonderingly closes the second stanza by saying it would *be/Profane to think thee any thing but thee* (19–20). This is the language of Christian theology and worship: to worship God is to know him for who He is.

- In several poems Donne uses conceits drawn from the practice of religion. *The Canonization* and *The Relic* develop the idea that the lovers are like saints in that they represent a pattern of what true love is. The poems work with such force that we might wonder whether Donne is doing more than work with the conventional idea that love is a kind of religion.

- Donne is troubled by unfaithfulness or inconstancy (see *Holy Sonnet 19*). Even the exuberantly buoyant *The Anniversary* contains the word *Treason* (26). In *Holy Sonnet 14* he says that *Reason* – God's *viceroy* in him – proves to be *weak or untrue* (8). John Carey, speculating about Donne's abandonment of Catholicism for Anglicanism, detects in his verse a *perpetual worry about fidelity and falseness*. Perhaps the guarded prickliness of *Woman's Constancy* discloses a fear that lovers are prone to be unfaithful.

- In his blending of the sacred and the profane, Donne might be searching or aspiring for what lies beyond worldly appearances. The subject of *The Undertaking* is finding *loveliness within* (13). It might even be that the search for *a woman true, and fair* (*Song: Go, and catch a falling star*, line 18) is, for all its apparently merry cynicism, a search beyond the world for what is pure.

The above points are about the content of Donne's poems. There are also continuities of style and manner between love and religious poems.

- In both kinds of poems the poet adopts an argumentative stance. Many of the love poems are poems of persuasion. But there is a problem: the poet's *masculine persuasive force* (*Elegy 16*, line 4) might work with a beloved, but not with God. This is particularly so when the poet is trying to persuade God to do what God has already done. At the close of *Holy Sonnet 7* he asks God to teach him how to repent, adding that *that's as good/As if thou hadst sealed my pardon, with thy blood*. But it is not a matter of *As if* for, according to

Christian doctrine, God has already sealed his pardon with the blood of Christ. Perhaps the line works precisely because the poet, desperate to repent, makes such an inappropriate request.

• Both the love and the religious poems are concerned with the poet's self. (Try counting the personal pronouns – *I, me, my, mine.*) Both love and religion are concerned with need. The lover needs the mutual assurance of the beloved's love as well as the satisfaction of desire. The lover of God has an even greater need – the salvation of the soul. It may be we should value the religious poems, because they are so honestly open about that need.

Religion

Religious language features in many of Donne's poems. As might be expected, the religious poems contain references to the Bible, to Christian tradition and to theology. The consequences of the Old Testament story of the Flood are mentioned in *Hymn to God my God, in my Sickness* (20), and *Good Friday, 1613. Riding Westward* uses the story from St Matthew's Gospel about darkness and earthquakes at Christ's crucifixion (19–20). The sickness hymn plays with the ancient idea that the cross of Christ stood in the same place as the tree in the Garden of Eden. There is a moment of controversy in *Twicknam Garden*, when the distraught lover presses into service the Catholic doctrine of transubstantiation to suggest that the distress of unrequited love changes *manna* (bread) into the bitterness of *gall* (6).

Donne and God

What kinds of religious thinking and feeling are expressed in Donne?

• Most readers will be struck by Donne's honesty and intensity. In *A Hymn to Christ, at the Author's last going into Germany*, he says openly and fervently: *if thou car'st not whom I love/Alas, thou lov'st not me* (23–4).

- Yet although we might judge the feelings as unusually intense, the religion itself is not unusual. He does not write about dramatic conversion or moments of spiritual illumination. Helen Gardner wrote: 'Donne, though in many ways a remarkable human being, is not remarkable for any spiritual gifts or graces which we recognize as at once extraordinary and beyond the experience of mankind.'

- The range of the poetry is narrow – sin and salvation. Sin, whether it be deliberate acts or the fallen state inherited from Adam, is alienation from God. The depth of this alienation is so great that only through the death of Christ, God's Son, can there be salvation. This fundamental Christian doctrine is present in Donne through his vocabulary: words such as *death*, *fear* and *despair* indicate sin, and *repent*, *delivery*, *purged*, *pardon*, *blood* and *grace* the salvation that rescues mankind.

- Salvation is often seen in what Christian theology calls an eschatological or apocalyptic perspective. These terms refer to the four last things – death, judgement, heaven and hell. *Holy Sonnet 6* sees judgement in highly individualistic terms. The poet casts himself as an actor in the *last scene* (1) of a great drama. In *Holy Sonnet 7* the Last Judgement is more communal with *numberless infinities/Of souls* (3–4) rising from their graves. It is not easy to know what Donne feels: is it fear and dread, or is there a strange thrill in the face of the final tumult?

- Religion often employs the language of paradox. Statements are made that seem self-contradictory but which, upon further thought, reveal deeper ideas. Jesus taught that he who loses his life shall find it. *Holy Sonnet 14* climaxes on a series of extreme paradoxes. The poet will never be *chaste* until he is (sexually) *ravished*. Donne might have felt that human experience – the competing demands of body and soul – have a paradoxical quality. He may also have enjoyed the verbal ingenuity of paradoxes.

- It is worth asking whether the imagination at work in the religious poems is Catholic or Protestant. The Church of

England, of course, is not a Protestant body, but in Donne's day it was strongly influenced by the ideas of Luther and Calvin (see Context, p. 10). The earnest inwardness of Donne's religious meditations might suggest the dramatic individualism of Protestantism. But, equally, this can be found in contemporary Catholic spiritual writing (see Context, pp. 10-11). What is more certain is that his imagery, particularly his imagining of the Last Judgement, owes a great deal to late medieval Catholicism.

Interpretations through language

The living voice

Donne sounds like no other poet. This is largely due to his language having the characteristics of everyday speech. In a Donne poem there are:
* quickenings of pace
* clusters of heavy stresses
* surprising cadences
* sudden changes in tone
* interruptions of rhythmic patterns
* variations in line length
* groupings of monosyllabic words
* short rhyming couplets
* a high proportion of verbs.

F.R. Leavis famously said that we read Donne 'as we read the living'. And a living voice is what we hear – urgent, passionate, purposeful, concerned and intellectually engaged.

Activity

What is the impact of the living voice in following lines?

> For I am every dead thing   *A Nocturnal upon S. Lucy's Day,*
> *being the shortest day* (12)
> Nothing else is.   *The Sun Rising* (22)
> I joy, that in these straits, I see my west   *Hymn to God my*
> *God, in my sickness* (11)

Discussion

The stress that falls heavily on the first syllable of *every* and then on both *dead* and *thing* slows the pace of the line and creates a mood of bleak finality. *Nothing* is assured, so we are prepared for the gritty affirmation of *is*. The word *joy* stands out as an expression of delight that helps to give the monosyllabic line a steady purposefulness.

Drama

Because we hear a living voice in Donne's poems, he has been compared to a dramatist. Dramatists of the day – Marlowe, Shakespeare, Webster – gave their characters lengthy speeches, which revealed intentions, motivations and turbulent emotional lives. How true is this also of Donne?

Another aspect of the drama of Donne's poems is that they imply a story or narrative leading up to the situation in which the poet speaks. Readers often have to piece together the story and imagine the drama of the situation. The drama of the situation is often strong in the love poems, and though immediate circumstances are less vivid in the religious poems, we are invited to imagine narratives leading to the utterances in *Holy Sonnets 13, 14, 17* and *19*. The consequences for the reader is that we have to learn to hear the speaker, to put ourselves in the position of the auditor or listener and, in some cases, picture the physical circumstances in which the encounter between speaker and auditor takes place. The narrative element and the immediacy of the encounter explain why Donne's poems are sometimes said to be dramatic monologues. Although this term is usually applied to nineteenth-century poems, such as those by Browning and Tennyson, the defining features of a situation, a person who is addressed and a revelation, not necessarily intentional, of the speaker's motives and mind can be found in some of Donne's poems.

Activity
What is the situation and what do we glimpse of the poet in *Woman's Constancy*?

Discussion
We are given two pointers as to time. She has loved him *one whole day* (1), and the poet anticipates that she will leave *Tomorrow* (2). Most of the poem is taken up with his rehearsal of what she might say. This discloses quite a lot about him. He is intellectually agile. His arguments are exact, and he enjoys playing with polarities: *you/Can have no way but falsehood to be true?* (12–13) The poet entertains us, but a reader may well wonder whether he is the one who has problems with constancy.

Openings

The drama of a Donne poem is usually most evident in the opening. To be a reader of Donne is, in a special sense, to be a listener. The poet speaks to the listener, and the reader overhears. When Leavis drew attention to the living – the contemporary – quality of Donne's voice, he was thinking of the opening of *The Good Morrow*:

> I wonder by my troth, what thou, and I
> Did, till we loved?

The poet wakes up to a love so authentic that it changes *thou* and *I* into *we* and judges his past loves as nothing but desire. The impulse of the line hurries the reader on to *Did*, at which point there is the delighted discovery that what either of them *did* in the past (we must recognize the sexual connotation) is surpassed in their new world of love.

Activity

What kind of impact does the opening of *Holy Sonnet 13* make?

Discussion

Because the sonnet starts with a question, the reader has to imagine the circumstances that have forced the poet to think in these terms. In the added emphasis of *this present* we feel the pressure of events or ideas that have led him to contemplate the end of time. The ordinary words for time *present* and *last night* alert us to the unnerving strangeness of everything we commonly accept as normal suddenly ceasing.

Perhaps Donne's poems sometimes fail to live up to the drama of their openings. (The ends of the poems can sound low-key and even nonchalant.) This is, in part, because the experience captured in the opening is a spur to thought, so the rest of the poem is an exploration of the significance of the experience. We should also remember that, formally speaking, openings are often more telling than the rest of a work. Musical openings are often more memorable than what follows.

Rhythm

Many of Donne's lines are rhythmically irregular. Either the stress does not come when the reader expects or it is very much heavier than expected. Take these two lines from *The Triple Fool*:

> Grief brought to numbers cannot be so fierce,
> For, he tames it, that fetters it in verse.   (10–11)

The first line approximates to the iambic pattern of much

English verse – an unstressed syllable followed by a stressed one. But there are questions: is *Grief* stressed as well as *brought*? In the second line, does the rhythm depart further from a regular sequence? Must we stress *For* because, as in everyday speech, it introduces a reason? Should we stress *tames*, thereby further disturbing the iambic rhythm?

Donne has long been notorious for the irregularities of his lines. His contemporary, Ben Jonson, said that for not keeping accent (being rhythmically regular) Donne 'deserved hanging'. He has been called harsh, licentious, rough and abrupt. Yet, as C.A. Patrides points out, Donne could write with measured fluency. Think, for instance, of *Song: Sweetest love*. Moreover, we could not hear the roguish departures unless there was a basic regularity. We must conclude that Donne *chose* to depart from regular rhythms.

Hearing Donne

It is often said of poetry that it blends sound and sense. The reader has to listen, for meaning is heard. Literary critics often talk not just of sounds but of sound values. This is truer of Donne than of many poets. The very sounds of the words express the strenuous logic of his arguments and the turmoil of his feelings.

Listen to the argument he frames in *A Fever* about the nature of the fire that will burn the world at the end of time:

> Oh wrangling schools, that search what fire
>   Shall burn this world, had none the wit
> Unto this knowledge to aspire,
>   That this her fever might be it?   (13–16)

We can hear in the snappy precision of the last line, the exactitude of the poet's thinking. And perhaps, too, there is a certain pleasure in both his discovery of the idea and the deftness with which he expresses it.

As to the expression of feelings through the sounds of his

words, the haunting opening of *The Expiration* achieves an appropriately lamenting verbal music:

> **So, so, break off this last lamenting kiss**

You may wish to think about how the long and short vowels give voice to the grief of parting lovers.

Activity

What is the effect of the sound values of these lines from *Air and Angels*?

> So in a voice, so in a shapeless flame,
> Angels affect us oft, and worshipped be   (3–4)

Discussion

The sounds embody the subject matter. The succession of 'o' sounds in the repeated *so*, and the long 'a' *in shapeless flame,/Angels* might be understood as the sound of a mind reaching for and then glimpsing the angelic creatures elusively present in a flickering flame.

Cadence

A cadence is the movement of sounds – their rhythms and pitches – towards the end of a line, clause or sentence. As cadence is a feature of spoken language, this is another way in which Donne's poetry comes close to everyday speech. Mood finds expression through cadence. Thus those of *Love's Growth* are light, joyful and eager. The cadences of the questions in *Hymn to God the Father* are so dark and subdued that there is a question whether the voice falls rather than rises. One particular cadence is characteristic of Donne – the rising note of triumph. Listen to the close of the first stanza of *The Anniversary*:

> Only our love hath no decay;
> This, no tomorrow hath, nor yesterday,
> Running it never runs from us away,
> But truly keeps his first, last, everlasting day.　　(7–10)

The cadences are steady and assured. There is no sense of decay, no drop in the voice, when the line closes on *decay*. The voice rises with the cadence on *away*, and this prepares the reader for the soaring cadence of *first, last* (the ordinary span of time) and then a sudden sweeping upward movement to the crucial and climactic *everlasting* (beyond time).

The movement of thoughts and feelings

If all the features of sound are considered together, we see that these material aspects of the poetry embody or enact the meanings and emotions of the poems. To read a Donne poem is to go on an emotional and intellectual journey in which we hear the poet thinking and feeling his way through an experience. Donne's poetry conveys the living experience of what it is to think and feel.

Activity

Describe the changes in thought and feeling expressed in these lines from *The Flea*:

> Oh stay, three lives in one flea spare,
> Where we almost, nay more than married are.　　(10–11)

Discussion

This is not just thinking; it is the experience of feeling one's way through a thought. In trying to prevent his beloved from killing the flea, the poet, with particular emphasis on *three* and *lives*, firmly asserts that they are *three lives in one flea*. He then tentatively chews over an idea. The word *almost* is slightly separated from *Where we*, and the first syllable bears the stress associated with someone realizing he is making an important distinction. Then in the long caesura (pause), a more compellingly certain thought strikes him. The word *nay* enacts the moment when he sees that in the flea they are *more than married*.

The love of argument

Argument is a particular form of movement. One of the features (or perhaps faults) of Donne is that significant experiences usually set him thinking. Thinking often increases the pace of a poem, and related to pace is compression. Under the pressure of urgent thought, Donne's style often becomes elliptical; that is, words are omitted. The result often puzzles readers. What exactly, several readers have asked, does he mean by *Let sea-discoverers to new words have gone (The Good Morrow,* line 12)?

But beyond puzzlement what most readers sense is his delight. Think about how words that scaffold arguments – *if, but, then* – are frequently delivered with an incisive thrust. There is an audible delight in getting an argument clear, Listen to the second stanza of *The Undertaking*:

> It were but madness now t'impart
> > The skill of specular stone,
> When he which can have learned the art
> > To cut it, can find none.

The delight consists in getting something said with pithy clarity. The movement of the stanza climaxes on *cut*. Can we hear in that word the pleasure he takes in the precision with which he has *cut* or clinched his argument?

Verbal play

Donne also takes delight in the multiple meanings of individual words. The term 'verbal play' stands for all the ways in which Donne enjoys the words with which he works.

Thomas Docherty points out that there is a linguistic aspect to the undressing the poet presses the woman to do in *Elegy 19*:

To his Mistress Going to Bed. In the order *Off with that girdle* (5), the poet might be enjoying not only his hopes of seeing the naked girl beneath her clothes but, on a linguistic level, the word 'girl' hidden in the word 'girdle'.

Puns

Donne might be said to flaunt his puns. Some are merrily indecent as in *country pleasures* (*The Good Morrow*, line 3), and some both indelicate and cleverly contemporary as when his roving hands explore the *new found land* of her body (*Elegy 19: To his Mistress Going to Bed*, line 27). The word *Newfoundland* dates from 1585. In *A Jet Ring Sent* he suggests a pun, surely with a feeling of gratification, on the French word *jette* – to throw: *fling me away* (8). We should remember that puns were common in sixteenth- and seventeenth-century literature. Shakespeare is full of them. Donne was forthright in his use of the pun, at one time he is said to have punned on his own name when he and his new wife were in financial distress: *John Donne Ann Donne Undone*.

Activity

What is to be made of the puns on his own name and possibly that of his wife, Ann More, in the repeated lines from *Hymn to God the Father*:

> When thou hast done, thou hast not done,
> For I have more. (11–12)

Discussion

There is no easy way of coming to terms with these puns. Should a man who knows his soul is in danger trouble himself, his reader (and God!) with a pun? A defence might take the form of the pleasure of possession. As he took pleasure in possessing his wife, Ann, so, the poet hopes, will God in possessing him.

Language as subject

As a poet who is aware of the range and power of language, it is not surprising that Donne sometimes makes language his subject matter. This happens in at least three ways:

- Donne often writes of speaking. The climax of *The Apparition* falls on the topic of speech. Having pictured the lurid details of his woman in bed with her lover, he pointedly says: *What I will say, I will not tell thee now* (14). At the close of *Hymn to God my God, in my Sickness*, he thinks about the text of the sermon he will preach to himself: *Be this my text, my sermon to mine own* (29).

- Love is also a matter of speech. The climax of *The Undertaking* involves talking about seeing *Virtue attired in woman* (18). The would-be lover has to dare to love that *loveliness within* (13) and *say so too* (19).

- Donne is aware that language can prove inadequate. *The Relic* closes with this admission:

> but now alas,
> All measure, and all language, I should pass,
> Should I tell what a miracle she was.   (31–33)

The note is distinctly religious. Donne is saying that as language fails when we try to speak of God, so the miracle of the beloved passes beyond the bounds of the sayable.

Two critical terms

Two terms are regularly used in critical discussions of Donne. Wit identifies a quality of mind, and conceit a feature of his figurative language.

Wit

Wit was (and still is) a term used to characterize Donne's originality and ingenuity of expression. It was the term used by Donne's contemporaries. In a poem probably written in 1610,

Ben Jonson spoke of Donne's *early wit*, meaning that from his youth Donne was an accomplished poet. Wit has the following features:

- Thought is concentrated, as in *A Valediction: forbidding Mourning*, where *refined* (17) picks up the association of *elemented* (16) to pithily present their love as virtually being of a different substance from that of ordinary lovers.
- Thought is imaginatively agile, making arresting comparisons. The comparison in *Twicknam Garden* between the power of love to devastate and the transubstantiation of the elements into the body and blood of Christ in the mass is as strikingly original as it is theologically outrageous.
- There is, as often in Donne, a knowing pleasure in getting ideas both firm and surprising. In *A Fever* he says that scholars debating the nature of the fire that would burn the world at the end of time:

> had none the wit
> Unto this knowledge to aspire,
> That this her fever might be it.   (14–16)

This is a piece of smart boasting. The scholars did not have the wit to see what the poet can. His mind, like the flames at the end of time, can *aspire* to the truth that her *fever* (hot like fire) might mark the end of the world. His wit also captures the sad implication that for him her death may well be the end of his world.

Conceit

A conceit is a far-fetched comparison which, surprisingly, draws attention to similarities between apparently very different objects. It was a common feature of sixteenth- and seventeenth-century poetry, owing much to the influence of the Petrarchan tradition (see Context, pp. 15-16). In Donne it has the following characteristics.

- It is often presented as an idea that has suddenly occurred to the poet. Note, for instance, the way conceits erupt into a poem without introduction. Very little prepares us for the conceit in *Air and Angels* of *love's pinnace* (18) – a swiftly moving ship.

- Yet there is a jesting element in the introduction of a conceit that presents the extraordinary comparison as something obvious. It obliges the reader to say: why didn't I think of that myself? The word that introduces the odd as obvious is 'as'. Arguing for a return to the body, the poet of *The Ecstasy* says that *As our blood labours to beget/Spirits* (61–2). The notion of spirits in anatomy was that they connected body and soul. There is, therefore, some sort of connection, but the language of anatomy is hardly an obvious way of making it.

- The above example shows us that a conceit surprises. The comparison is unusual, even far-fetched. A conceit should jolt the reader and prompt an investigation as to how apt it is.

- Perhaps Donne's facility for establishing a comparison through a conceit is more memorable than his construction of an argument. Readers find they can recall the oddity of a conceit but find it difficult saying exactly how Donne uses it in an argument.

- And perhaps, also, some conceits do not work. Are we only left with strangeness rather than truth? The intellectual status of the conceit is often problematic: is this mere verbal cleverness or are we given an insight into the world? Can we apply to Donne what Dr Johnson said of Abraham Cowley: 'thoughts are often new, but seldom natural'? Johnson's judgement on conceits was: 'heterogeneous ideas yoked by violence together'.

- A conceit is extendable. It takes the two opening stanzas of *A Valediction: forbidding Mourning* to compare the quiet death of virtuous men with the parting of true lovers. Tracing the several points of comparison makes reading a Donne poem a series of imaginative journeys.

- There is only so much life in a conceit. It is as if Donne is often distracted by the possibilities of his own language, and when that language, so to speak, wears itself out, another comparison attracts him. After the death of virtuous men, *A Valediction: forbidding Mourning* moves on to conceits on earthquakes, astronomical tremblings, the nature of substances and gold leaf till it reaches the compasses.

- What we can learn from his use and abandonment of comparisons is that Donne's conceits are 'local'. They illuminate the idea he is dealing with at a particular stage in the poem. We do not have to treat them as a key to the whole poem.

Metaphysical poetry

Donne (and later poets such as Herbert, Marvell and Crashaw) is often called a metaphysical poet. The term goes back to Dryden, who wrote that Donne 'affects the Metaphysics', meaning that he introduces philosophical and scholarly issues into his poems. By the twentieth century, the term came to be used of the features commonly associated with the poetry of Donne and his later followers. Thus the following points characterize metaphysical poetry.

- There is a dramatic sense of the poet in the poem. The poet is present in arresting openings, the changing contours of feeling and the purposeful arguing.
- The rhythms and sounds of the poem approximate closely to the patterns of everyday speech, marked by outbursts of feeling and thoughtful hesitations.
- There is a conscious delight in intellectual cleverness, often in the form of verbal play.
- The attitudes of the poet are often abrasively cynical, bitter, jesting or dismissive.
- There is a love of intricate argument and a delight in paradoxes.
- The imagery is drawn from a wide range of academic fields. This gives the poems an intellectual, or scholarly, thrust.
- The images are often outlandish. The reader has to struggle to see the appropriateness of what is being said.

- The range of topics is wide, and often several subjects intertwine. In Donne's poems emotions range from the exuberant pleasures of love to burdened meditations on mortality and sin.

Poetic forms

In Donne's day poems were crafted into lines and stanzas. The lines were sustained by regular or near regular rhythms, and the stanzas given shape by rhyme schemes. Some poetic forms (the obvious example is the sonnet) achieved a fixed and, in terms of rhyme, flexible form, while lyrics (poems that either have the qualities of song or were intended to be set to music) were written in a variety of forms.

Donne, like his contemporaries, wrote in sonnet form. The *Holy Sonnets* use the rhyme scheme of what is usually called the Petrarchan sonnet – an eight line section (the octave) concluded by a section of six lines (the sestet). These sections are given form by having a distinctive rhyme scheme. There is often an important change in thought and feeling between the octave and the sestet. *Holy Sonnet 13* opens with the poet asking with something approaching horror whether *The picture of Christ crucified* (3) in his heart is one that will *adjudge him* unto *hell* (7). The sestet begins with the firm cry: *No, no*. By way of warning, it should be said that not all the *Holy Sonnets* have such an emphatic break between octave and sestet.

Donne's love poems are collectively known as the *Songs and Sonnets*. The title is a broad one, intended, no doubt, to indicate that these are lyrical poems about affection, longing and passion. It is often observed that they do not contain sonnets in the formal sense. However, C.A. Patrides has pointed out that the stanza form of *Air and Angels* is a free variation of the sonnet with sestet preceding the octave.

The Elegies are something of a puzzle. The term usually denotes a lamenting or reflective poem, but while this might be said of *Elegy 5: His Picture*, it can hardly apply to the roguish boasting of *Elegy 4: The Perfume*. It looks as if Donne adopted the title because of the form of the poems. They are written in rather rough and conversational rhyming couplets. He might have been following Marlowe's *Ovid's Elegies* (some were published in 1599), which translate Ovid's Latin into rhyming couplets.

A feature of the poems in *Songs and Sonnets* is that they display a mastery of a very wide range of stanza forms. For instance, *A Fever* is written in expertly precise quatrains (stanzas of four lines) while the stanza form of *Lovers' Infiniteness* is eleven lines long. Most critics agree that this is not just a matter of formal experiments. Donne creates distinctive rhythms as expressions of his particular subject matter and, similarly, shapes his stanza forms according to what he is saying.

Interpretations through critical issues

Donne and the critics

The remarks above about stanza form and subject matter have the ring about them of what has become 'traditional' literary criticism. The inseparability of form and content is the bedrock of much academic literary study. As Thomas Docherty points out there is an historical aspect to this. When literary studies were established after the Great War, the poet who both prompted thinking and was a touchstone of what literature could do was John Donne. He embodied the admired quality of blending what he said with the way he said it. The insight was not new. Earlier thinkers commented on the indissolubility of form and content. J.H. Newman was one and Coleridge, a critic as well as a poet, another. Interestingly, Coleridge was a great admirer of Donne.

Reason and emotion

In 1921 a passing remark in a review by T.S. Eliot supplied some terms that still influence thinking about Donne. He says of

George Chapman, an Elizabethan playwright, that

> ...there is a direct sensuous apprehension of thought or a
> re-creation of thought into feeling, which is exactly what
> we find in Donne.

He goes on to say about Donne:

> A thought to Donne was an experience; it modified
> his sensibility.

'The poetic sensibility', as Eliot says 'could devour any kind of experience'. Many readers were introduced to Donne by way of these interpretations. Generations were told that in Donne there was a remarkable fusion of thought and feeling. Is there?

There is a strong pulse of feeling in the thought of the first stanza of *Love's Growth*. The poet finds that:

> Love's not so pure, and abstract, as they use
> To say...   (11–12)

This seems to issue from the experience of a lover, who has discovered that what people *use/To say* is not true. That colloquial phrase – an off-hand conversational gesture – shows the feeling in the thought. But is this always true of Donne? Should we, for instance, value *The Undertaking* for its fusion of thought and feeling?

Activity

How does the first stanza of *Song: Sweetest Love* measure up to Eliot's idea that for Donne a thought was an experience?

Discussion

Do the words *But since* mark a shift from thought impelled by feeling to what might just be a 'bright idea'? You may, however, feel that there is feeling here – delight in a new idea.

The wrong key?

Donne has long attracted the attentions of critics, who are also poets. The passage from Dryden quoted above in the section on metaphysical poetry continues with the comment that in his love poetry he 'perplexes the minds of the fair sex with nice speculations of philosophy, when he should engage their hearts, and entertain them with the softness of love'. What Dryden touches on is the issue of whether Donne's love poetry is in the wrong key. Is he too concerned with ingenious arguments?

Activity

How consistent is the poet's concern for his beloved in *A Fever*?

Discussion

The tender concern of *Oh do not die* is touchingly sincere. He does what many people do: plead as if recovery were entirely up to the one who is sick. But when he confidently says *But yet thou canst not die, I know* (5), do we wonder whether he is becoming absorbed with the idea of her breath as the spirit of the world? Perhaps, however, this bright little thought is a way of distracting himself from an overwhelming anguish. Readers might also wonder what the significance is of the change in the fifth stanza from second person (*thee*) to third person (*she*).

The pleasures of love?

When we remember that Donne's love poems circulated in hand-written form long before they were published, we may guess that one of the pleasures of reading him was that he boldly took on erotic topics. *The Dream* deals with the act of love, and there are frequent plays upon sexually ambiguous words. It must be admitted that many readers find such writing exciting.

Yet it can also be slightly puzzling. Though Donne can be so openly sexual, do we sometimes feel that the scenes are, so to speak, fully lit, and the poet views all with fixed and defiant stare?

His language might be said to hold things at a distance. Is the effect of such language erotic? Furthermore, there is an interesting absence. What exactly do we learn about the experience of love? To put the point bluntly: can we learn from Donne what soft human flesh feels like? Consider the famous *Elegy 19: To his Mistress Going to Bed*. C.S. Lewis said that it was 'intended to arouse the appetite it describes'. But how sensual – and therefore appetizing – is it? Does Donne appeal to any sense other than the unblinking eye? And even that scrutinizing eye does not tell us what she looks like. As Joan Bennett said of *The Undertaking* in an article replying to C.S. Lewis: 'Donne tells us very little about that beauty of "colour and skin"'. Donne does ask her to allow his roving hands to explore her naked body, but there is nothing in the poem to suggest that he actually does so. Perhaps that pleasure (like many of the other pleasures of love) is felt only in the imagination. Is it only his mind that roves?

Beloveds

One of the critical strategies we have learnt in at least the last forty years is how to read literature from a female perspective. Donne writes of *my words' masculine persuasive force* (*Elegy 16: On his Mistress*, line 4), but we are not usually made to understand what it must feel like to be the object of such force. His beloveds are mute, and when they do speak, what they say is indirectly reported by the poet.

Activity

Imagine *Elegy 5: His Picture* from the perspective of the woman who is addressed.

Discussion

She may well be comforted by the assurance of the second line that her picture will dwell in his heart. But what might she make of the long passage (5–10) on his possible appearance after his journey? Lines 11–12 might be read as crucial. Is his chief concern that she will see the point of those whom he calls *rival fools*? And what might she feel about being given the 'correct' response: *Do his hurts reach me* (14)? The end of the poem is also problematic. Does she need the analogy of babes being fed on milk?

The language of exploitation

Those interested in how women might respond to Donne's poetry will not overlook these lines from *Elegy 19: To his Mistress Going to Bed*:

> O my America, my new found land,
> My kingdom, safeliest when with one man manned,
> My mine of precious stones, my empery,
> How blessed am I in thus discovering thee!   (27–30)

The woman's body becomes a new colony, owned and protected by the invading power and exploited for its wealth.

More might be at stake here than feminism. This might be read as an early example of colonial literature; literature, that is, that betrays the attitudes of those who acquired foreign lands for their own use. It might be said that this reading ignores the wit of a poet who can make such an inventive connection. In reply, it might be said that such wit is there to conceal the reality of exploitation.

Love poetry?

It is not surprising that many readers have wondered whether Donne's work should even be called love poetry. Love, they might claim, involves a concern for what the beloved is thinking and feeling. How often do we find Donne concerned about the heart and mind of the other? Because the auditor (the one who listens) is silent, the reader can only imagine what she (and in one case, he) is thinking.

There is no easy way of sorting out this issue. The number of different attitudes indicates that Donne liked writing about the varied drama of love. Some of these little dramas work precisely because the poet attempts no sympathetic engagement. An obvious example is *Love's Alchemy*. Yet there is also the grammatical transformation of *thou* and *I* into *we* in *The Good Morrow*, an indication, surely, of mutual love. And certainly the imagery of their faces reflected in their eyes beautifully enacts an equal, loving response. Would it be wrong to point out that this is what the poet thinks?

We should not forget *Break of Day*, the poem in which a woman speaks. Or does she? How different is this voice from the loud male ones?

Metaphysical, moral

One critic, Helen Gardner, questioned whether 'metaphysical' is quite the right term for Donne. Her view is that he explores metaphysical ideas not for their own sake, but for the light they throw on his true subject, the heart of man. She called this interest a moral one, moral not in the sense of the rights and wrongs of behaviour but a probing of human nature.

Such a statement raises the very interesting question of Donne and truth. Does Donne introduce ideas not because he regards them as important statements of how things are but because he can use them as metaphors or analogies of what it is like to be human? Perhaps, because they were being undermined, traditional ideas about the world were valued less for their truth and more for their poetic usefulness.

Activity

How should we understand the ideas about nothingness in the second stanza of *A Nocturnal upon S. Lucy's Day, being the shortest day*?

Discussion

The rough meaning of lines 10–18 is that by a new chemical process the essence of nothingness has been extracted from the poet. (There is a full discussion in Theodore Redpath's edition of the *Songs and Sonnets*.) The idea of extracting essences is derived, as Donne's language makes clear, from Alchemy. Yet do we have to believe or even accept that Donne believed in Alchemy in order to feel the sadness of this falling cadence: *For I am every dead thing*? Such a line tells us about the human heart without committing us to a belief in Alchemy.

Strange, true

Conceits, we may suppose, were intended to be surprising. The reader expects the poet to serve up a comparison that, at least at first, is astonishing. Whoever, we might think, would want to compare lovers who are apart yet united in terms of the *stiff twin compasses* (A *Valediction: forbidding Mourning*, line 26)? Love is intimate, warm and emotionally yielding; compasses are hard and cold. Perhaps there is a problem here. We expect conceits to be strange, and yet, after consideration, true. But are they always like that? We might sometimes find ourselves saying: this is strange rather than true. This is not an issue that can be settled by argument alone. Readers of poetry are people, and people react differently. In fact, the same person can react in different ways on different occasions. What we should remember is that responses are significant. Those who find truth in Donne's puzzling conceits are committed to saying that he is a poet who tells us something, either about how things are or the human condition. Those who find him strange will have judged the poetry as only revealing what Donne was like.

Sincerity or art?

It might be misleading to consistently treat Donne's poems as outbursts of deeply felt passion. Perhaps there is an element of playfulness. Do we feel that in *Love's Alchemy* Donne delivers his diatribe against love with a pleasurable gusto? To get the rhythms and inflections of irritated disgust right is a matter of art. If, as has been assumed, there is the attempt in many of these poems to create a dramatic situation out of which the poet speaks, then Donne will have been concerned to get the manner of speaking right. He need not have felt the feelings he expresses, and in that sense, need not have 'meant' what he said. Yet is it possible to keep separate sincerity of feeling from the discipline of shaping works of art?

Activity

Is *A Valediction: of Weeping* to be enjoyed for its expression of feeling or the artistry of its language?

Discussion

There is a touching urgency in the opening. Furthermore, the last line of the first stanza voices the distress of separation. But is this true of the masterful intricacy with which Donne explores the conceit of the mapmakers? The concise summary of making everything out of something that represented nothing is so deftly executed in *And quickly make that, which was nothing, all* (13) that we hear, above all, the pleasure in the art of argument. But finally, we should ask who would want to exclude sincerity from the last lines? If these lines do convince us as expressions of deep feeling, this might be because Donne's art moves from *thou and I* to the more measured recognition of an objective mutuality in *Who'er sighs most, is cruellest, and hastes the other's death.*

Well wrought urns?

Cleanth Brooks singled out Donne's phrase *a well wrought urn* (*The Canonization*, line 33) to signify his own idea of a poem as a highly organized structure, held together by a complex of ironies and energized by paradoxical thinking. (Should we also ponder on the fact that this image of art is a funeral urn?)

It is worth asking in the light of this what kind of poems Donne wrote. They are carefully crafted and, also, held in tension by a series of contrasts and balances. And they refer to the making of art and artistic objects. *The Triple Fool* is about the poet hearing his own art mediated through another art – music. Images of artistic objects include the weeping statues in *Twicknam Garden*.

But they can be described in other ways. Do the poems themselves matter more than the exploratory reasoning that often dominates the middle sections? The way the poems move from topic to topic suggests the growth of a plant rather than the processes whereby an urn is formed. Donne adjusts and adapts his thoughts and feelings, discovering himself as he thinks. His poems might, therefore, be said to be organic.

Love and love of God

A final issue is the problem frequently encountered in Donne: to whom is the poet speaking? The audience of the love poems is the beloved; God is the audience of the religious poems. But to whom is he the more attentive? The reader may well feel that at times the lover is so fascinated by his own thinking that he forgets his beloved's presence. But does the poet forget God? One way of reading *Holy Sonnet 14* is that it is the poet who batters with his demands and heartfelt declarations. Listen to the imploring confirmation of his feeling: *Yet dearly'I love you* (9). Is he ever quite so openly passionate with his *profane mistresses* (*Holy Sonnet 13*, line 10)?

Try testing out Helen Gardner's words: 'His maker (God) is more powerfully present to the imagination in his divine poems than any mistress is in his love poems.' Might it be that Donne's most intense love poetry is that addressed to God?

Conclusion

The following remarks are intended for those who are writing about Donne.

- You should try to convey Donne's delight in his ingenious thinking. Try to bring out the art by which he draws the reader into the twists and turns of intellectual debate.
- One of the delights of Donne is the movement of thought and feeling. When we talk about the dramatic quality of his verse, one of the things we are drawing attention to is the way each poem is a kind of story, a series of emotional / intellectual events that add up to something of interest and importance.
- When writing about Donne, try to bring out the range of his learning and the purposes to which he puts it. Remember that learning often shows something about how people think and feel.
- Never forget that he is a poet of his times. The excitement of learning in an age when knowledge was uncertain gives a dangerous edge to what he writes.
- It is a good idea to handle the critical language associated with Donne. Words such as 'conceit' and 'metaphysical' can help us think through what Donne's work is like.
- An element in the drama of Donne is his verbal music. The exquisite blends of sounds in a line are not only beautiful but enact the thoughts and feelings of the words.
- Remember that there are many moods in Donne. He can be darkly serious as well as funny.
- Learn to value the moments of insight into the poet's heart and mind. You may find more of these in the religious poems.
- Always keep in mind the exciting uncertainty of interpreting him. This is an alluringly teasing body of poetry.
- Finally, never forget your own responses. Donne is a writer who provokes us into engaging with his ways of thinking and feeling, so what you feel about him is an important part of that engagement.

Essay Questions

1 In what senses was John Donne a poet of his time? Consider this question with close reference to at least **three** of the set poems.

2 Discuss the different ways in which Donne uses partings and journeys in his poetry.

3 Consider the importance of learning and intellectual excitement in the poetry of John Donne.

4 How should we describe John Donne's religious temperament and outlook?

5 Is the poetry of John Donne more concerned with divine than human love?

6 What do the love poems and the religious poems of John Donne have in common?

7 Consider the view that there runs through John Donne's poetry a preoccupation with the relationship between the body and the soul.

8 Is Donne consistently a poet absorbed by the thought of death?

9 'Donne's presentation of the theme of love is extremely varied.' Discuss this statement with close reference to at least **three** poems.

10 Do you find Donne to be chiefly a poet of the joys or the miseries of love?

11 Do you think it is possible to divide Donne's poems between the sacred and the profane or do many poems deal with both areas of experience? Make detailed reference to at least **three** poems in your answer.

12 Select at least **three** of Donne's poems and consider how the rhythms, sounds and cadences are appropriate to the subject matter.

Chronology of Donne's life and times

Events in Donne's life

1572   Born in London into a Catholic family.

1576   Death of father.

1584   Starts his education at Oxford. Because he was Catholic, he was not allowed to take a degree.

1588-9 It is possible that he studies at Cambridge.

1591   Begins law studies in London. Reads widely in theology and possibly writes some of the *Songs and Sonnets*.

1593   His brother, Henry, is imprisoned for hiding a Catholic priest in his house. He dies in Newgate prison.

1596   Takes part in the expedition to Cadiz (Spain) when it is taken and looted.

1597   Sails on the 'Islands' expedition. Later he is a member of an expedition to the Azores. On his return he becomes secretary to the Lord Keeper, Sir Thomas Egerton.

Historical events

1576   Building of the first theatre in London.

1577-80 Drake circumnavigates the world.

1587   Execution of the Catholic Mary Queen of Scots.

1588   The Spanish Armada is defeated. One of its aims was toleration for English Catholics. Probable date of Shakespeare's first play, *The Comedy of Errors*.

1591   Publication of Sir Philip Sidney's *Astrophel and Stella*, a sonnet sequence written according to Petrarchan conventions.

1595   Sir Walter Ralegh's voyage to Guiana.

1599   The Globe Theatre is opened by Shakespeare's company of players.

1601	Becomes an MP but takes no part in debates or committees. Secretly marries Ann More, then under 21.
1602	Imprisoned for the secret marriage, dismissed by Sir Thomas Egerton, and, when released, lives in Pyrford, Surrey. *The Sun Rising* and *The Canonization* may date from this period.
1605	Travels on the Continent. Visits Paris and may have visited Venice. Returns in 1606.
1606	Moves with his growing family to Mitcham, Surrey.
1607	Takes lodgings in the Strand while seeking a public office.
	Establishes a firm friendship with Lucy, Countess of Bedford, who moves into Twickenham Park. *Twickenham Garden* may date from this period. It is probable that most of the Holy sonnets were written between 1607 and 1611.
	Bishop Morton urges him to be ordained as a priest. He declines. He probably assists Morton in religious controversies, arising from the Gunpowder Plot.
1609	*The Expiration* is published in Ferrabosco's *Airs*.

1600	The East India Company is formed. Essex rebellion against Elizabeth I fails.
1600–1	Probable date of Shakespeare's *Hamlet*.
1603	Death of Elizabeth I. James I becomes King.
1603–4	Plague is very severe in London.
1605	The Gunpowder Plot fails. As a result the loyalty of Catholics to the State becomes a controversial issue.
1609	Publication of Kepler's work confirms that the earth revolves around the sun.

Events in Donne's life

1610   *Pseudo-Martyr*, a work of religious controversy directed against Catholics, is published. Donne is awarded an honorary Master of Arts (MA) by Oxford University.

1611   He travels with Sir Robert Drury on the Continent, staying at Amiens and Paris. His departure may have prompted him to write *Song: Sweetest love* and *Valediction: forbidding Mourning*. When he returns in 1612 he lodges in Drury House, Drury Lane, where he remains till 1621.

1614   Sits in Parliament, serving on four committees.

1615   Ordained priest. Becomes a royal chaplain and receives a Doctor of Divinity (DD) from Cambridge University.

1616   Preaches at Court. Becomes Reader in Divinity at Lincoln's Inn.

1617   Preaches at Paul's Cross, a famous pulpit in the grounds of St Paul's Cathedral.

       His wife dies after giving birth to a stillborn child. She was 33 and had borne 12 children, 7 of whom survived her.

Historical events

1610   Galileo's *Sidereus Nuncias* again confirms that the sun is the centre of the solar system.

1611   Publication of the Authorised Version of the Bible.

1616   Death of William Shakespeare.

1619	Appointed chaplain to Lord Doncaster's embassy to Germany. Writes *A Hymn to Christ*. Visits Heidelberg, where he preaches. Returns in 1620.1620
1620	A portrait painted.
1621	Elected Dean of St Paul's Cathedral and preaches there on Christmas Day.
1622	Resigns as reader in Divinity at Lincoln's Inn. Two sermons are published.
1623	Seriously ill; probably writes *Hymn to God my God, in my Sickness* and *A Hymn to God the Father*.
1625	Preaches at court to Charles I.
1628	Ill from August to October.
1630	Makes his will.
1631	Dies and is buried in St Paul's.
1632	Memorial statue erected in St Paul's.
1633	First *Collected Poems* published.

| 1625 | Death of James I, Charles I becomes king. |
| 1628 | William Harvey's *De Motu Cordis* establishes the theory of the circulation of blood. |

Further Reading

Texts

Donne is not always an easy poet, so critical editions with explanatory notes are very useful and, in some areas of study, essential. The following provide detailed notes and, in some cases, introductions.

The Elegies and the Songs and Sonnets of John Donne, edited by Helen Gardner (Oxford, 1965)

The Divine Poems of John Donne, edited by Helen Gardner (Oxford, 1952)

The Complete English Poems of John Donne, edited by C.A. Patrides (Everyman, 1985)

The Songs and Sonnets of John Donne, edited by Theodore Redpath (Methuen, 1956)

John Donne: The Complete English Poems, edited by A.J. Smith, (Penguin, 1971)

Biography

R.C. Bald: *John Donne: A Life* (Oxford, 1970)

John Stubbs: *John Donne: The Reformed Soul* (Penguin / Viking, 2006)

Criticism

The Cambridge Companion to John Donne (C.U.P., 2006). Essays on the whole range of Donne's work.

John Carey, *John Donne: Life, Mind and Art* (Faber and Faber, 1990). This is full of ideas and boldly integrates poetry and biography.

Thomas Docherty, *John Donne, Undone* (Methuen, 1986). A study of Donne in the terms of contemporary critical and interpretive interests.

Gerald Hammond (ed.), *The Metaphysical Poets* (Palgrave, 1974). This collection includes the important essay by T.S. Eliot.

J.B. Leishman, *The Monarch of Wit* (Hutchinson, 1951). This is a clearly written study of Donne's literary achievements.

Julian Lovelock (ed.), *John Donne* (Palgrave, 1973). A collection of essays in the Casebook series.

Louis l. Martz, *The Poetry of Meditation* (Yale, 1954). This is a classic study of Donne's (and other poets') dependence upon traditions of religious meditation.

Joe Nutt, *John Donne* (Palgrave, 1999). A discussion of the poetry in the Analysing Texts series.

A.J. Smith, *John Donne: The Critical Heritage* (Routledge & Kegan Paul, 1975). This complete record of critical comments on Donne up to the end of the nineteenth century includes the remarks of Dryden, Johnson and Coleridge.

Richard Sugg, *John Donne* (Palgrave, 2007)

Index of Titles and First Lines